Aver of ge
Aggression

Safe work in services for adolescents and young adults

Second Edition

Owen Booker

Russell House Publishing

First Edition published in 1999 by:
Russell House Publishing Ltd.
This Second Edition published in 2004 by:
Russell House Publishing Ltd.
4 St. George's House
Uplyme Road
Lyme Regis
Dorset DT7 3LS

Tel: 01297-443948
Fax: 01297-442722
e-mail: help@russellhouse.co.uk
www.russellhouse.co.uk

British Library Cataloguing-in-publication Data:
A catalogue record for this book is available from the British Library.

ISBN: 1-903855-44-6

Typeset by TW Typesetting, Plymouth, Devon
Printed by Antony Rowe, Chippenham

About Russell House Publishing

RHP is a group of social work, probation, education and youth and community work
practitioners and academics working in collaboration with a professional publishing
team.
Our aim is to work closely with the field to produce innovative
and valuable materials to help managers, trainers, practitioners
and students.
We are keen to receive feedback on publications and new ideas for future projects.
For details of our other publications please visit our website or ask us for a catalogue.
Contact details are on this page.

Contents

Introduction   1
    What risk?   1
    Safety at work   1
    Who is at risk and where?   3
    The consequences of inaction   8
    What this book offers   9
    Who this book is designed to help   13
    How to use this book   14

Section One: Working with Angry People

Chapter 1 **Responses to Aggression**   19
    Personal reactions to aggression   19
    What to do in a situation   22
    Context   27
    The CARMA© model for managing distressed persons   28
    Professional response   30
    The professional in a situation: activity one   35

Chapter 2 **Interpersonal Immediate Techniques**   41
    Ignoring (1)   41
    Proximity and touch control (2)   44
    Signals (3)   47
    Involvement and interest (4)   48
    Injection of affection (5)   50
    Humour (6)   52
    Appeal (7)   53
    Saying 'no' (8)   54
    Hurdle-help (9)   56
    Permitting (10)   57

Chapter 3 **Wordy Techniques**   60
    Acceptance and interpretation (11)   60
    Mapping (12)   63

Chapter 4 **Managing Techniques**   66
    Restructuring (13)   66
    Bouncing (14)   68
    Regrouping (15)   70

Avoiding a void (16) 71

Promises and rewards (17) 73

Punishment, consequences and threats (18) 75

Physical restraint (19) 79

Section Two: The Organisational Environment

Chapter 5 **The Physical Environment** 83

The built environment 83

The living environment 84

Control of the environment (20) 84

Controlling the setting (21) 88

Chapter 6 **Health and Safety Matters** 93

Health and safety law 93

Safe practice 95

Safe systems 96

Sick record case study 101

Effect of violence on the self 103

Chapter 7 **Organisational Culture** 105

Professional context 105

Professional review: activity two 105

Workplace and espoused theory 107

The cultural constructs 110

- Nicknames (1) 110
- Scapegoating (2) 112
- Collusion (3) 115
- Balance (4) 120
- Pathology and style (5) 124
- Letting time work (6) 130

Chapter 8 **Personal Health** 133

The personal constructs 133

- Silence and paraphrasing (7) 133
- Watch your step (8) 135
- Self-monitoring (9) 138
- Personal development contract (10) 143
- Getting more for self (11) 144
- Self-esteem concepts applied (12) 148

Contact Information 151

References 153

Dedicated to the peace makers among us

Acknowledgements

John Woodward from whom I learnt much about self and others.
John Lampen, and John Visser for their work on early first edition drafts.
And all those whose thought, anecdote, experience and example I have drawn upon to add substance.

About the author

Owen Booker has had over 30 years experience within childcare, therapeutic and mainstream education, in the LA, independent and voluntary sectors; and from reception classes to tertiary education and youth work. The children and young people worked with have included those whose behaviours have represented some of the most significant and disturbing difficulties. He has led the work of teachers, residential care and social work staff. For a period he was a director of a Therapeutic Community within the Charterhouse Group.

He is an Advocate Representative with the Voice for the Child in Care, working for young people in secure accommodation; and has been a Lay Assessor with the Social Services inspection of residential care homes.

Owen's freelance work is centred on improving the potential of people through conflict reduction. He provides consultancy to a variety of care and education organisations, independent professional supervision, line manager training, and personnel training for work with young people with challenging behaviour. He also retains some employment within a LEA Behaviour Support Service, working with parents, children and schools.

Organisations of which he is member include The Society of Education Consultants, Human Scale Education, The Caspari Foundation, SEBDA, The Social Care Association, and The Howard League.

Contact via web site: www.pptc.co.uk

Preface

This second edition, with new content and a reorganised presentation, provides improved focus and more detailed information, including new illustrative case material (e.g. Sick Record Case Study, Chapter 6).

Two chapters have been added which expand the scope of the work to cover environmental factors (Chapter 5) and health and safety issues (Chapter 6).

There is also a greater emphasis on the physiology of aggression and several key issues including Risk Assessment, Workplace Culture, and Quality Assurance are now given a higher profile. Particular prominence is given in Chapter 1 to the professional responsibility for ensuring that personal actions are properly considered, and that well-being and legal consequences are taken into account.

Averting Aggression still remains a personal practical guide for everyone whose work can require them to deal with aggressive behaviours; in social or youth work, education, residential care, youth justice, the police, prison, probation, and health services. It offers advice, knowledge, skills, techniques, and contact information. It presents a unified approach that allows personal practice and the workplace generally to be scrutinised, and recognises that service systems as well as personnel, must at times take responsibility as the source for the aggression met in clients and service users.

People in their teens and twenties have the greatest incidence of violent and aggressive behaviour, and it is ironic that we all have the highest hopes for these young people at the portal of their productive lives. However, the human potential for personal change – and for interpersonal conflict – respects no barriers of age, or of race, gender, or ability. Whomever you work with, this book will give you:

- CARMA®, a conflict reduction model for response to an angry person.
- 21 proven techniques to safely divert or diffuse and reduce aggressive behaviour from any source.
- Practical ideas to improve safety, minimise sources of anger, manage others, and protect people from harm.

In your work, you and your colleagues may never intentionally be aggressive *yourselves*. But you can inadvertently work against positive processes if the challenges of stress, bullying, or similar dysfunctional forms of difficulty are not met effectively. This book will help you and your colleagues to:

- Make effective risk-assessments.
- Determine that your workplace is psychologically healthy.
- Guard against beng drawn into aggressive operations.
- Ensure that everyone, including you, is properly valued.

Introduction

What risk?

When considering conflict within contemporary society as a whole, most of us will start out with one of two viewpoints. They contrast considerably!

- One view is that people live more civilised lives compared with other times or other places. The closest most people come to actual violence is on the TV screen or in the paper. It can seem that violence saturates us, but this is simply the efficiency of modern reporting. Statistically, actual numbers of incidents are very few and the chances of personal involvement slim. Violent incidents, even in public places, are generally prevented by effective methods of social care, and the security afforded by modern policing.

- The alternative view is that everyone is at risk of a confrontation and attack in the home, at work, and in the street. The risks include mugging, road rage, persons influenced by drink or drugs, or with mental health problems; and gunmen amok: Yardie drug dealers, kids robbing stores and petrol stations, and asocial persons with grudges. And the new horror of international terrorism. Everyone either knows of somebody who has been involved in violence, or has a personal story to tell.

The truth probably lies somewhere in between, but is hard to define precisely. Aggressive behaviour does seem to be on the increase, but only broad agreement is found as to what degree. Some statistical sources suggest overall there is no bulging trend of violence. The 2001–2 British Crime Survey reported a total of just a little less than three million reported violent incidents, and showed an increase only in the number of actual wounding. This will resonate with those who believe that there is less hesitation by offenders to use weapons such as knives and guns. However, the relevant figures are complex and differ from police recorded crime, which is subject to new reporting procedures. Current police figures do show an increase in violent crime. The level of aggression directed to people at work, however, is alarming.

Safety at work

After a period of decline in the number of attacks on people at work, there has been an upturn. The rate of violent assaults at work more than doubled between 1981 and 1991, representing over 13 per cent of all assaults (British Crime Survey, 1992), and the trend begun in that decade shows no sign of abating. Health and Safety Executive (HSE) research indicates an order of 1.2 million violent incidents to employees in England and Wales each year, and 40 million working days lost. The 2000 Crime Survey figures (for 1999) gave 1.3 million incidents of violence to people at work, with 634,000 physical attacks.

Deaths that are work related (in any way) have fallen greatly consequent on better measures for health and safety; these are now 0.9 per 100K employees a year in the UK. But assaults at work have more than doubled – to over 13 per cent of all assaults. In 2001–2 a Public Accounts Committee report on one sector only, noted 95,000 incidents of violence against NHS staff and care workers, a year later the DoH's own survey reported 116,000 incidents of violence across all their organisations. The Health and Safety Commission currently estimates that one in five workers have been physically attacked or threatened by members of the public. Drink, drugs, and mental health problems lie behind most attacks (at 65 per cent; 15 per cent; and 15 per cent respectively). Although it is unclear whether increased frequency is a result of actual occurrence or greater readiness to report, violent and aggressive behaviour is routine experience in some occupations and in some specific situations. Violent and aggressive behaviour happens daily in places such as police stations and psychiatric units; and on Saturday nights in particular, in hospital accident and emergency centres.

One suggestion to explain the upturn is that the public are much less willing to accord unconditional respect to public servants. Pressure on services can show as professional indifference to those who had expected better service whether this is medical attention, a school place for their child with special needs, prompt emergencies response, or a cleaner street. The public relations profile of many servants has also been lowered by a series of scandals across a number of services including police, care, health, and education.

There are also signs to suggest that people generally are more likely to find fault with legitimate denial, see insult or abuse where none was meant, or act out anger for flimsy reasons. We see the evidence for this by exceptional incidents in situations where conventionally there has been little association with extreme violence. For example, schools have featured in the media recently. Incidents have ranged from a Shropshire dinner lady attacked by a gang of pupils, to a number of affrays that have involved stabbing (at least eight in 2003, of which three have led to death), and examples are a London teacher slashed in the face by a teenage pupil, and the 14-year-old pupil stabbed to death by a schoolmate in Birkbeck School, a small rural school in Lincolnshire. Lamentably, the scale of the problem in schools in England and Wales is difficult to ascertain, as there is no central register of incidents available to collate LEA data (Scotland began this in 1997 with beneficial outcomes).

Threats and violence at work will cause people going about their duties in a reasonable manner to hesitate for fear of innocently triggering unwarranted reaction. This is particularly so in places or situations where distressed people are concentrated or where authority is confronted. Interpersonal conflict is routine to some degree for many at work. Although this may be part of the job they are paid to do, it is always true that those who are carrying out this work are ordinary people, with families, fears, hopes, and aspirations.

This book will help to make your work safer from aggressive behaviour, and particularly by showing how aggressive incidents may be averted in the first place. It is written from the viewpoint that the skills and knowledge that avert aggression can be learned, and this will help a great many people: professional, service users, and society as a whole.

Who is at risk and where?

- **The Health Service** illustrates the degree that aggression impinges upon a public service. Currently about 1 in 20 nurses can expect some form of physical assault each year. Concerns began to emerge strongly in the mid 1990s. In 1996 it was reported that a third of health service staff had been affected by violence at work (*Nursing Times,* 1997: 7.5; 93.19). A contemporary survey by the BBC and *Nursing Times* found that nearly all staff working on Accident and Emergency at some point had been verbally abused, and that close to half of all staff had experienced actual physical harm with 56 per cent of the incidents reported occurring during the survey year (*Here and Now*, BBC1, 12.5.97). On a Saturday night in a busy A and E unit, pleas may not impact on hard-working staff operating a triage system, and aggression, no matter if from frustration or drink, will seem a shortcut to notice and attention. Elsewhere the service deals routinely with people who are genuinely distressed or with mental health difficulties. The government has been determined to protect NHS staff and NHS trusts should have systems in place to minimise the numbers of violent incidents. The most apparent outcome to the public is a hardened line towards transgressors backed by publicity and information; illustrated for example by the universal use of posters in reception areas to inform about the policy on abuse to staff – always one of zero-tolerance.

- **The Police** are expected to exemplify operational skill and interest for public order, and successfully control people who threaten to upset the peace. Yet police actions are increasingly questioned. The service has faced repeated calls for public accountability on a range of events and issues, and been confronted with evidence that parts of their work are flawed. This ranges from accusations of institutional racism, to questions about custody procedures when yet another person dies in a police station (41 per cent increase overall in the four years 1996–2000; 65 in 1998–9). Different police authorities do have different reputations. A number are working hard to develop more sensitive policing and new expertise, particularly in the recognition of adults with learning difficulties. Other examples are the return to localised community policing and improved recognition of domestic violence. Operational changes are resulting in different forms of intervention that require officers to have a higher order of interpersonal skill and a better understanding of psychological factors than has hitherto been expected. All this is not before time, as one in nine police and security staff are assaulted each year.

- **Social work**. If the police and health professionals are in the front-line, social workers are not far behind. Concerns for their safety have grown rapidly, again since the mid 1990s. In 1996–7 more than 500 social workers were so injured they had to take three or more days sick leave, and between 1980 and 2000 seven staff have been killed (HSE data). In 1998 Unison dealt with over 200 claims for criminal injury compensation. The government's own *National Task Force on Violence Against Social Care Staff* reported in January 2001. It found workers in social care and health settings eight times more likely than the average employee to experience physical attack, half of all social care staff aged under 40 had been attacked, with three in five for all male staff. It has set a target to reduce violence to social workers by 25 per cent by 2005 (DoH task force report, *A safer place*; www.doh.gov.uk/violencetaskforce). The periodical Community Care recently and unusually, relegated client issues in favour of directly championing a stand against violence at work for its social work readers. The 'No Fear' campaign was given impetus by the death of Jenny Morison in 1998. It also commissioned a survey. This found that nine out of ten social workers felt at risk of violence while doing their jobs, with 50 per cent suffering high levels of stress. This is not surprising. Social workers are used to conflict as a considerable amount of their work is tantamount to policing people who would prefer they were left alone. And it is lone workers who are most often doing outreach and community work. Unfortunately public sympathy and confidence in social services continues to be eroded by some controversial events and from repeat scandals – particularly concerning child-protection; and in a more low key but ongoing manner concerning residential child care, and the treatment of adults with learning difficulties. Invariably inquiries result in common elements of blame that include inadequate monitoring, sub-plots of reluctance to report on clients, too little training, and areas of unsatisfactory support and practice of which a common outcome is timidity when faced with aggressive persons.

- **Residential care** is a special case. It is a poorly paid sector, has the longest hours, is least supported by management, and relies most on insufficiently qualified staff; yet has to meet high demands. The National Institute for Social Work reported that residential workers are most likely to be attacked, particularly if clients have mental health difficulties, or are children or adolescents (*Community Care*, 1998, 22.7). The National Task Force (see 'Social work' above) reported incidences of physical attack affecting two thirds of all residential workers.

- **Residential childcare.** A key expectation of the *Quality Protects* initiative included that placement changes will reduce for children in public care. Those offering residential childcare face higher expectations to remain committed to children with difficult behaviours and to succeed with them, yet residential social workers (RSWs) are invariably in situational conflict with their clients. This is because their clients are predominantly teenagers with challenging behaviours; and who are also passing through the developmental period recognised for its potential for conflict. RSWs have to impose external demands and expectations, and bring each young person successfully forward with little more than the strength of their personal relationship. Whether they work in a family group home, in crisis intervention, or in a busy and volatile secure unit, these care workers frequently go home carrying both physical and emotional bruises as a result of their duties.

- **Prisons for young offenders (YOI)** predominantly house young men aged 15 to 21. In 2002, there were 2,500 of these young men in the lower age group 15–17 (figures from Howard League). Aggressive behaviours are expected in YOIs, as this age and gender group gives and receives more violence than any other, and perforce of sentence are selected for their criminal behaviour. Inmates harm staff, each other, and themselves. The risk is high for inmates to self-harm, or be bullied to the point of committing suicide (18 children in YOIs have killed themselves over the past decade). The need to maintain order, as well as endeavouring to help individuals with their problem behaviours makes conflicting demands upon prison workers and their methods. This counters against prisons offering safe and therapeutic environments. The HM Chief Inspector of Prisons has generally been very critical of the YOI estate (*The Howard Journal of Criminal Justice,* August 1999, 38.3: 347). Similarly, Secure Training Centres have found their work confrontationally difficult as well as controversial. The issue of harm to children aged 16–18 in prison service custody is unresolved. Between April 2000 and January 2002 there were 3,620 instances recorded of force used against children in custody, resulting in injuries to 296 children, five of whom needed hospital treatment.

- **Prisons for adults.** Adults convicted of criminal acts, like their younger counterparts show limited emotional development, and have poor life opportunities. Research by the Basic Skills Agency (website, 2002) indicated one in two prisoners have literacy difficulties, and that there was a correlation between this difficulty and frequency of police intercession in their lives. The prison population is growing (currently 125 per 100,000 citizens, and 72,000 persons in 2002) and the Home Office predict a 50 per cent rise in prison population by the end of the decade. A number of prisons have had very critical inspections. The Howard League again points to suicides as 'an indictment of the whole penal system'. In 2002, 94 adult prisoners committed suicide, the highest number since records began; this was 116 per 100,000 prisoners compared to 89 per 100,000 the year before. It is imperative that pressures on the service does not also mean that inmates are managed in ways that compound rather than help address their difficulties. A prison is perhaps the epitome of the closed institution, and can present an environment where abuse can most flourish without good systems and the right people to work within them.

- **Probation Services** have been operating under difficult conditions with uncertain funding yet high expectations. There has been a recent history of redundancy and early retirement in a demoralised service. The requirement for a social work qualification has been abolished (1991 Criminal Justice Act). Probation and bail hostels accommodate offenders whose profiles are often far more serious than those of inmates in local prisons. Careful and expensive supervision is essential to ensure conditions are not broken, and for sex offenders especially, reintegration into community is fraught with difficulties and essential to manage well. Probation officers have to be supportive in the manner they confront the dysfunctional behaviours of their probationers to avoid their recidivism, manage re-introduction so as to not alarm local communities, induct less qualified staff, and all on less money.

- **Youth Justice.** The present government is keen to improve public order and civic responsibility, and improve the life chances for youth. The 1998 Crime and Disorder Act placed increased responsibility on the youth justice system to contain and prevent anti-social juvenile behaviour. Youth Offender Teams (YOTs) work pre-emptively with young people to keep them out of serious trouble. The teams are composed of people drawn from different services, and early team development experienced difficulties associated with this. Their work is bolstered by the recent legislation for Child Safety, Anti-Social Behaviour, Child Curfew, and Parenting Orders. Although the implementation of these legal powers is quite disparate one area from another, there are now larger numbers of children, young people and parents confronted for their poor observance of societal norms. Most of these people have lived lives freer from intervention before, and many resent what they view as intrusion into their lives.
The other pressure on the service concerns young people coming back into the community, and how well they are supported. The Howard League reported (*Sentenced to Fail*, 1998) that of 66 young people aged 15–19 and released from prison, only five of them had received help from a youth justice worker to prepare for their release. The concern remains how best to ensure appropriate support to prevent re-offending, and how to ensure that youth justice workers undertake supervision work positively and not view it as extended punishment.

- **Youth Work** is also greatly financially restrained within most local authorities, despite that the media and local councillors make much of incidents that involve groups of young people behaving badly. Under age drinking, substance abuse, criminal activity, gang type cliques, and alternative cultures can flourish where youth work is not effective. Some young people have always sought dysfunctional ways to gain personal significance. It is now recognised that these problems affect small country towns and rural areas as much as inner cities. Youth work relies upon outreach contact in the locality; this is demanding, sensitive work, and workers do not have the immediate support of colleagues on hand if threatened. Significantly, young men aged 16–24 years are most at risk of experiencing violent crime (British Crime Survey 2001–2:16.2 per cent within the age group).

- **Educational Services**
  Schools can experience considerable problems of aggressive behaviour. Inclusion for all pupils means the continued enrolment of disruptive pupils, despite this being a contentious issue; support services, and the number of associated initiatives are growing. The publication of school performance on exclusions and other criteria has provided evidence to highlight that schools often do not have sufficiently sensitive pastoral and special needs expertise, or locally there are particular unmet social or economic problems that impact upon schools. The profession is facing a high pace of change, a judgmental inspection system, and league table comparisons. These all put stress on schools staff. Assault to teachers (by pupils and parents) is a phenomenon to the degree now that claims for injury compensation are no longer novel, and it seems more regularly there are incidents when teachers assault pupils. Pupil behaviour remains a high profile issue highlighted by union surveys (principally NASUWT); these also point to the growing involvement of female pupils in physical conflict. The TUC Report 1: *Preventing violence at work* ascribes the rate of assault to education workers generally in any one period at 14 per cent, other research suggests a 1:56 risk.
  Tertiary Colleges find cadres of students are no longer deferential to the college environment or the opportunities presented. Whether or not these students are actually worse behaved than formerly, there is a very considerable expansion of student numbers that is impacting on facilities. This will include statistically more young people with mental health difficulties, with other behaviour problems, or substance abuse. The government's current 14–19 Strategy intends that tertiary colleges (along with their vocational courses) will also cope with the considerable addition of young people disaffected from secondary education.

- **Other professionals** who encounter aggressive members of the public in their daily work (and occasionally orchestrated attacks) include: ambulance medics, fire fighters, security staff, publicans, transport industry workers, social security staff, and reception personnel.

Whatever the actual situation for your workplace, threat and violence do appear to be more readily acknowledged by those caught up in it. Generally there is a greater willingness to report incidents, and tolerance is reducing. This is demonstrated by the greater vociferousness of the media, and the opinion of unions and local communities. And despite some controversy about the use of anti-social behaviour orders (ASBOs), there is now more legislation and government guidance in support of a safer society. For example, soon after the 'No Fear' campaign (see Social Services above) the government launched its own plan to reduce violence to social services and DoH personnel; one recommendation was that employers establish a baseline with a target of 25 per cent reduction by 2003. Most authorities have produced new guidelines.

One result of the contemporary focus on violence in society is distinctions are depicted more clearly. Distinctions between people may be illustrated by the difference between violence from those who are not fully responsible for their behaviour, such as the elderly and confused, and persons with mental health difficulties, and persons who make more deliberate use of violence. It has also become very clear that young men both suffer and cause more violence than any other gender or age group. Men are much more likely to directly act out anger than women, despite a new propensity for them to do the same, as the growth of so-called 'ladette' behaviour illustrates.

Similar distinctions between different environments prompt a level of awareness that assists recognition of the types and sources of conflict. For example, the operational focus necessary by personnel in institutions where it is routine to deal with particular forms of aggressive outburst, compared to the growth of safety awareness that has come about as we navigate our thinking through the wider range of violent behaviour represented generally across society. Some issues remain in tension, for example, the degree that the freedom of potentially dangerous people (of all kinds) has become more difficult to restrict without good justification; and the universal risks associated in all the public places and spaces that we all frequent.

For employees, many difficulties remain constant. Dangerous or threatening people of all kinds are met with in retail, public, and corporate services. Too many employers still drag too slowly on making proper audit or recognition of the risk potentials, and have yet to update or even make necessary responses. Problems include poor recognition of the general case, and a reluctance to make risk assessment without the push of prior incident, and inadequate training. Generally, whatever their work is, too few employees are routinely given sufficient and well-targeted training of good quality. Too often training emphasises operational action without sufficient work to underpin understanding of the causes of violence. Certainly many employees and workplaces handle conflict well, but without knowing how to reduce it in the first place.

The consequences of inaction

There can be dire consequences when conflict and aggression becomes frequent, but those in authority respond inadequately:

- Employers will see absenteeism and staff turnover increase.
- Employees will experience low morale and lose professional self-regard.

- Organisation costs will increase:
  - Insurance premiums and legal fees will rise (from dealing with events, and from staff claims for compensation).
  - More appointment and training work associated with high staff turnover.
  - Performance will be reduced.
  - Marketing image will be damaged.

What this book offers

At this point you may be asking if your work, or organisation, fits into this kind of situation, and whether you would benefit from this book? The answer is yes if aggressive behaviour ever occurs at your work-place, and definitely if this is routinely the case. You may be an employer or manager with responsibility for staff or client safety, or yourself wish to understand better why acts of aggression occur in order to improve your practice, or reduce your personal vulnerability.

This book will:

- Add to the necessary knowledge base that promotes prevention.

- Remind managers of the relevant Health and Safety legislation.

- Inform the process of risk-assessment.

- Present practical ideas to safely reduce conflict and protect people from harm.

- Provide a conflict-reduction model (Carma) for defusing an angry person.

- Offer proven techniques to safely diffuse, divert, and reduce aggressive behaviour.

- Help you determine if your workplace is psychologically healthy.

- Consider workplace occurrences that are:
  - Common to many services and some service industries.
  - Not necessarily extreme events.

- Help you and your colleagues in your responses to problem behaviour.

- Promote your personal awareness, insight, and understanding.

Aggression manifests in two ways, interpersonal events, and as a result of the cultural environment.

Interpersonal aggression (Section One)

The most obvious is raw, individualised, person-to-person hostility, from a vitriolic stream of verbal abuse to murderous physical intent, and from one person or a group of people. Although the victim may not warrant the abuse, in that it is often displaced, the reason for it is usually easily uncovered.

Aggression within the environment (Section Two)

The second form of aggression has many manifestations, but it is likely to be faceless or hidden and subtler in expression. This results from bad practice of systems, methods, or ideology. It includes corporate or institutionalised aggression. Although there are victims and actual physical conflict, where the prime trigger for aggression originates may not be so clear, nor what drives it. Despite the obvious situations when a national regime is maintained by the violence and violations it sanctions, this scale begins with situations that arise in more commonplace and civilised cultures, and may involve otherwise caring people.

Who offers aggression?

Ordinary people

Aggressors need not be distressed or angry clients. Aggressors can be ordinary people like you or one of your colleagues. Ordinary people can act in extraordinary ways when they lose their temper. Our tolerance thresholds vary though life. Our health, the degree of stress, and our innate personality, can combine to produce moments when we act in ways that may be regretted later. The risk rises with people who carry special personal troubles, and with those whose insight into self and others is limited. This raises issues about the different levels of, and interaction between, emotional and intellectual intelligence, and the different life experiences of 'ordinary' people.

Organisations that seem dysfunctional and damaging invariably contain people who otherwise think themselves normal and considerate individuals. There is usually no intention to damage the chances or potential of others, but many people make harmful actions much more frequently than they might realise. It is surprisingly commonplace particularly in institutions of all kinds for others to suffer as a result of an 'ordinary' situation or 'normal' response.

Young people

Although aggressors may be of any age, children, teenagers, and young adults are the client group highlighted. This group includes young people with emotional and behavioural difficulties, mental health problems, learning difficulties, or histories of criminal convictions or substance abuse; these conditions all have association with physical violence. Children are the most likely client group to (only) threaten or verbally abuse staff; whereas people in their teens and twenties have the highest level of actual violence and most association with aggressive behaviour, and their difficulties show in a wider range of settings. Work in many of these settings will include coping with confrontation as part of a normal day.

It is also a matter of some national shame that we lock up so many young people instead of providing sufficient therapeutic or psychological intervention, and without sufficient recognition and treatment in instances when the child has mental health difficulties. Many of these young people suffer ill treatment. There are major issues emerging about the safe care and proper treatment of children in YOIs. The recent High Court judgement that the Children Act 1989 applies to children in prison custody has vague resolution and little operational impact as yet. The Social Services Inspectorate inspection late 2002 at the Medway Centre (STC) found children still locked away in single separation (solitary confinement) for long periods, and staff using racially offensive language such as 'half-caste', and 'coloured'.

Young men suffer, and perpetrate, more violence than any other sector of the population (75 per cent of all attacks are by males aged 14–26). There are over 11,000 young people under 21 who are currently held within the system of HM prison, YOI, STC, or within local authority secure children's homes (LASCH). The British Dyslexia Association has long indicated that up to half of young offenders (in YOIs) will have some form of specific learning difficulty giving rise to problems of literacy and numeracy (*The Reality of Dyslexia*, Osmond, 1995), others often have other learning difficulties. The link between aggression and poor educational attainment is emotion. Even mild learning difficulties can impinge on personality and cognitive behaviour in that sufferers misunderstand social interactions and the tiny interpersonal cues that people make. If you have poor emotional understanding of self and others you are more likely to get into trouble, and many young men who do, will continue so for the rest of their adult lives.

The ironic contrast to all poor practice is that we all have the highest hopes for these young people at the portal of their productive lives. It is with young people that there is most hope for change, and with whom human potential has still its greatest store. But although young people are a point of focus, the human potential for change, and for interpersonal conflict, has no barriers of age, or of race, gender, and ability; and this book addresses the general case.

People in your organisation

Corporate aggression is difficult to confront. People, within and without such organisations, suffer from misdirected and insidious power. Aggressive attitudes and expectations are invariably disguised. They are hidden within targets to be met, or kept from more open disclosure by the movement of personnel. An entrenched ethos of aggression can lie couched in the anxieties or culture of a group, and their high throughput may be rewarded with money and approval; this may ensure an easier task, or be a way of evading proper accountability. The pressures are always contemporary, despite that excesses may be formally recognised, recently for example, racism in the London Metropolitan Police.

Management styles do evolve, for example the 'hard-heart' of the 1980s has given way to a more sensitive approach to employer-employee relationships, but sometimes attempts to do well produce problems. Charters now abound to ensure rights, but new tensions have emerged as people and resources are put under pressure to meet new service levels. The charters raise the expectations of clients, and are a focus for demand by managers. The clash when there is a gap in the middle and everyone's expectations fall short can spill over into interpersonal conflict.

Institutional systems can produce aggressive responses because of inadequate resources, methods or procedures; this can have internal and external consequences. This may be illustrated by the continuous pressure on Local Authorities (particularly in the southeast) of the high influx of refugees and asylum seekers from the different conflicts of the past decade. Racist and bullying attitudes have been found in social services staff that led to inadequate provision for refugees (Save the Children report: *Community Care*. 1998, 19.11). The growth of resentment towards refugees among sectors of the population differs from area to area and seems to reflect how effective and how open local authorities are concerning refugee issues. The street incidents and disorder exemplified in Glasgow, Bradford and Wrexham over 2002–3 compares poorly to other areas that have more successfully absorbed similar numbers – such as Devon.

Pressure on systems is often accompanied by a focus of blame. Blame may either fall on the client whose vulnerability is exposed and tested, or on the worker who has to cope. This can often get passed along down the line, because bullying systems produce bullying people. Workplace bullying is now more readily recognised, but although managers who bully colleagues or clients may be easy to identify, this does not mean that they are easy to deal with. Alternatively, workers who dislike to compromise their professional principles will find the discharge of duties increasingly difficult, and find they carry a growing burden of unease.

Today, many of the old certainties seem to be in flux. Most professions have issues of political correctness that are shifting or being challenged; whether by movement or a directive (contemporary examples are the growth in awareness and legislation concerning disability, to the turnabout in government guidelines about restraint of children in care). Organisational change may be embraced or perceived as threat. For varied reasons some people will always continue to act in old ways and pay only lip-service to new codes of practice.

Changing consensus, and changing strengths of emphases, makes individual workers vulnerable, especially when dealing with clients who offer verbal or physical abuse. If very clear guidance is lacking, workers will act on their best interpretation, or upon their best sense of professional conduct. Ironically, on occasions when action is met by disapproval from a senior colleague this may illustrate the lack of consensus or practice guidelines. Workers will face accusations of over-zealousness, or inappropriate response. When repeatedly caught in this way, people lose drive. They eventually avoid risking censure by opting out of independent action. Their focus, and sense of professional self, becomes challenged and uncertain.

Situations that expose or test personal weaknesses can make anyone angry, frustrated, or anxious. But service users are the people most likely to be dysfunctional in some way, be carrying the most problems, and have the least personal resources or skills to cope. Their feelings are frequently expressed physically, and workers have to deal with the resulting conflict: made worse if they are caught up between service limitations and the needs or expectations of distraught clients (the 'gap in the middle').

Who this book is designed to help

The motivation for this book lies with sympathy and concern for all workers who engage with people who may have challenging behaviour, anger, or aggressive tendencies. Handling others who are distressed and angry is a most demanding professional expectation. As Goleman states:

> *If the test of social skill is the ability to calm distressing emotions in others, then handling someone at the peak of rage is perhaps the ultimate measure of mastery.*
>
> (Daniel Goleman, Emotional Intelligence: 124)

A non-emotional response to aggression in another may well control the person, but so will containment by walls or drugs. Responses that value the human condition are motivated by feelings of sympathy or empathy, and these exchanges invariably have a therapeutic influence. And not only is, 'emotionally an act of empathy a masterly tension reducer' (Goleman, 1996: 143), but the gaining of trust makes possible the beginnings of new actions and new beliefs.

Working with angry people

If your job sometimes involves responding to aggression face-to-face, this book will help you divert aggressive behaviour into something less damaging, both for the benefit of yourself and the other person involved. It may help identify where further training may be needed.

The work environment

There may be some practices at work that you are unhappy about, that operational outcomes or the manner of particular colleagues, actually contribute to client anger. You may similarly feel or actually be threatened yourself. Work may not progress as you think it should, or you feel at risk of professional compromise. Maybe aggressive clients only increase how angry you or colleagues feel? Such situations are not unusual from time to time in many work places, and may be comparatively permanent features.

Sometimes it takes new eyes or new courage to question practice. And questioning practice from time to time is itself good practice. This book will help you to focus if you have professional discomfort, to identify cause and suggest action; or help you review your practice. It may lead you towards other sources of assistance, or towards professional development. It will assist you to be empowered, and to act rather than react.

How to use this book

The two sections, *Working with Angry People* and *The Organisational Environment*, correspond to the two main sources of aggression I ascribe: interpersonal and environmental.

There is a training activity associated with each section. Each activity can be done alone or in a group, either or both will produce useful outcomes. Ideally each should be done at the point it is met when reading through (Activity One is relevant to both sections). I know that often these tasks are skipped. The choice is yours, but each activity is intended as preparation to bring forward thoughts and knowledge you may already have, and to signpost the issues the text that follows it will address. After reading each section you may wish to return to the activity for a rethink, to make comparisons with what you did before, or to add to your own conclusions. Repeating Activity Two may be especially productive if you have a supervisory responsibility.

Section One. Working with Angry People

Chapter 1 presents physiological and professional considerations, and offers model (with a mnemonic) for dealing with an angry person; it concludes with Activity One. The rest of the section presents nineteen interpersonal techniques or skills useful to reduce the likelihood and impact of confrontations. I recommend that the techniques are each considered for relevance to your work, and taken up only one at a time so they may be embedded in your repertoire of skills.

The techniques are subdivided into three types:

- Techniques for immediate interpersonal application – Chapter 2.
- Techniques that rely on talking – Chapter 3.
- Techniques to manage people and situations – Chapter 4.

Section Two. The Organisational Environment

This section is about systems, organisations, and you. Any technique in Section One – and generally how one may wish to operate – is very dependent on material factors in the work environment, and matters of health and safety. Chapter 5 concerns the Physical Environment of workplaces; Chapter 6 concerns Health and Safety matters, and matters of risk assessment run though both chapters. The two last 'techniques' are found in Chapter 5.

Chapter 7 is prefaced by Activity Two that provides a model for the evaluation of the workplace or an organisation's approach to the work undertaken. This is followed by some ideas related to quality assurance by the way they help differentiate between what your organisation intends and what it actually achieves. The remainder of the book presents twelve constructs for your reflection. These provide a checklist for psychological and organisational health, of the people and system you work within, and about you; and are split into two areas to reflect this divide:

- Organisational Culture – the second part of Chapter 7.
- Personal Health – Chapter 8.

If these constructs are of little benefit then I am pleased that you and your workplace are OK. But if it is not, you may find an answer, or a descriptor for the malaise you sense, or understand it better, and I hope I will have encouraged you to do something about it.

Section One:
Working with Angry People

Chapter 1

Responses to Aggression

Personal reactions to aggression

Physiology is the starting-point. We would not have survived as a species without the capacity for aggression in the face of danger. Anthropology and psychology have brought the associated mechanisms involved into most people's understanding, that is, the notion of 'fight, flight, or freeze' as instinctive reactions:

- Fight: as self-defence.
  The objective is to overcome the aggressor. Normally timid people can exceptionally be roused to a frenzy to ensure this – perhaps to protect someone they love. It can result in over-reaction or the inappropriate use of a weapon.

- Flight: to get away.
  Walk, run, or jump. This may well involve physical action that would not normally be considered, or work materials and possessions are left behind.

- Freeze: present no stimulus.
  Freezing is also a natural defence mechanism, it does not invite chase as flight may, and by avoiding fight it presents as submissive and protects from the probable harm of an unprepared defensive response.

In a confrontation a number of things can happen along a continuum of physiological symptoms, and these will occur to those involved whether aggressor or victim. With sudden and significant anger, or fear, blood flow to the body surface becomes restricted. The face pales, and the mouth may go dry, the person may be unable to speak or shout out, and normal powers of rational thought are overcome by more primitive brain functioning controlled by the amygdala (see Dawes, LeDoux, or Goleman). The amygdala act as a control centre. When alarmed they connect sensory input directly with parts of the brain used for action and bypass the areas used for reasoning and reactions become very autonomic. Breathing becomes shallow, and with anger, the face becomes suffused. In both instances, oxygen supply to the brain is lessened, and the ability to calmly sequence thought or respond to other stimuli is lessened.

People report a variety of sensations when tense or angry or otherwise with high emotional arousal, such as tunnel vision, seeing only the object of their attention, and sensitised hearing. Adrenaline rushes to the nerve endings, and fingers and toes tingle in preparation for a surge of physical activity, some compensation perhaps for depleted oxygen. The body floods with endorphins and injuries are received with lessened sensitivity to pain. Some body processes like digestion begin to shut down. An urgent need to use the lavatory may be felt. This is a relic of autonomic reaction when lighter body weight probably assisted quicker escape. Values appear to alter and even treasured possessions can be sacrificed in the passion of the moment, from throwing away something costly or valued, to an action that puts life at risk, either yours or the aggressors. People do produce surges of strength when stressed; this same superhuman power might be used for harm or good. Extraordinary feats are achieved – there are accounts of people lifting cars to free their trapped children.

Very aroused persons in a 'blind panic' can be a danger to innocent staff or bystanders, either in the belief they can resolve their problem, or reasoning they are seen to blame for an unforeseen turn of event they lash out unexpectedly, with words or actions. Others who get mixed up in the situation are usually unable to act before it impacts upon them.

An angry person can be taut, intense, and oblivious of anything except their point of focus, or they can be a ridiculous figure with contradictory, garbled words, or a squeaky, hesitant voice. Normal breathing and voice control is lessened, and making sense is compromised along with higher order thinking skills.

In this state of arousal people will make irrational connections, incorrect deductions, and wrong interactions concerning their immediate environment. A small movement may be interpreted as the start of an attack; a man in a uniform may be thought to be a policeman. Equipment will jam, phones will not work, doors not open, but the information mishandling that caused this will not be recognised in the panic of the moment, the person will instead create some other explanation.

Classic demonstrations of this phenomenon are often picked up on CCTV, and occasionally shown on Crimewatch type TV programmes. Criminals, already highly aroused, can do crazy things. A common error is the belief that doors just walked through can become locked because they seem not to open. They violently attack doors in order to escape, when the reality is they open the other way, but they have not been able to reason well enough to recognise this. One famous clip shows a criminal full face as he approaches a camera with a paint spray to block out its use.

When there has been stress arousal by an aggressive interchange, the body is left trembling. Much of this is the 'chemical aftershock' from the hormones that have surged through the body, and the person will most probably be unable to resume work immediately. Taking 'time out' to compose is the most advisable measure to assist with the personal state. Both parties are at risk of mishandling situations and returning to a heightened state unless time is allowed for the body to process the chemical charge. Going elsewhere for a period, for some fresh air, or to cool the face with a cold splash, allows the body to settle and the mind to assert better control. New emotions about self and the incident will have come to the fore with feelings of relief or frustration, which may be expressed with tears. A more peaceable place is valuable together with some time, reassurance, and comfort. The person should be offered a drink. The mouth and throat will be dry, and taking refreshment is not only reviving, it provides a distinct period for regaining normal emotions. Later, it is helpful if the situation can be talked through with someone impartial but supportive. A debriefing is especially useful to review the decisions and risk issues surrounding the event.

Confrontations experienced frequently at a low level are a major, but unrecognised source of stress, and can lead to eventual mental or physiological collapse unless good supervision or other support is available (see the Sick Record Case Study, Chapter 6). A repetitive state of alarm can cause a person to become highly sensitised to the source of their distress, and their ability for higher cerebral function in given contexts or environments may become impaired. Some behaviour may become quite automatic, and continue long after the original trigger source is gone. There are links here for why anxiety often spills out as aggression; it has similar physiological effects that impact upon body reactions and drive the person into defensive action.

The neurological work in the USA by Professor Bruce Perry and others illustrates this phenomenon well (see Perry). The research informs how growing up fearfully in chaotic or unpredictable environments affects the development of neural pathways and brain size of children. In infants and children who significantly lack a secure nurturing environment the prefrontal cortex (which deals with feelings and social interaction) is measurably smaller, and these children become hypersensitive to stress with overactive aggressive defence mechanisms. It is postulated this condition provides the predisposition for aggressive behaviour that many individuals continue with into adult life.

Serious or very intense events are more likely to be acknowledged and supported. High impact events, especially if one is unused to violence, will leave people physically and emotionally drained. Workers can be left feeling de-skilled and guilty (Chapter 7) and later they may have to deal with depression, or flashbacks if they suffer 'post-traumatic' episodes.

> A colleague and I once had to escort a young man on a journey in a car. I thought I
> knew him quite well, and the circumstances behind the journey had a long and
> complex history. I was driving, and my passengers were in the rear. The young man

suddenly attacked me from behind. The driving wheel was kicked from my hands, and I came close to losing control of the car as a determined assault was launched upon my colleague and me.

Once I had managed to stop, the situation was safer, but my colleague and I were barely able to contain the young man until the police arrived to assist. Everyone sustained some hurt and bruising. The car interior was considerably damaged, and the roof pushed up from the kicks it had received. The incident left me exhausted, shaking, and momentarily disabled. I got command of myself and got on with what had to be done. It became a long and trying day.

It was some days later as I drove along the same stretch of road that my unresolved emotions unexpectedly surfaced. I had to pull up, and I was unable to drive for a while. I had to recognise that my feelings and reactions had not been dealt with.

Do not underestimate the physiological and psychological effect that violence can have on you or a colleague.

What to do in a situation

Aggression not met with appropriate responses can help the aggressor to consider they have control of the situation and their demands or degree of threat increases. Bullying tactics rely on there being no challenge. In other instances, particularly when the aggressor has mental health or severe emotional problems, the aggressor may be looking for containment, or attention to, their out-of-control feelings. Delay in responding may increase their anxiety and allow them to believe that their actions are not significant enough, so they then adopt more desperate measures. Circumstances when a quick response would be effective and normally expected from the worker concerned, but not made, are potentially open to critical comment or allegations of professional incompetence. The following points relate to observing and deconstructing confrontations.

Antecedents and disruption

It is important always to remember that aggression always has an antecedent, it is a reaction to something that happened earlier. People who are 'captive' such as patients, pupils, or prisoners will often become disruptive when opportunity presents if they are made upset (typically bored, ignored, frustrated, or anxious). Most of us have some capacity to react unfavourably to unwarranted pressure or inconvenience.

Sometimes a small slight is the trigger to releasing deeper repressed feelings. When this occurs the explosion of emotion may not only be considerably removed from the source problem, it is often bewildering, overpowering, and violent in expression. This gives rise to the kinds of incidents encountered often in therapeutic community settings, and occasionally by on-call duty social workers and the police.

Some aggression is deliberately conceived as a coercive means to get what is wanted, or is broadly hostile in nature, and projected indiscriminately. Either way, once someone presents themselves in a vociferously angry manner, they are being disruptive, and at risk of further aggression if they are mishandled.

Angry people want a response, and they want it straight away. They want to see that their level of arousal is echoed in the degree to which others react to them. If disruption is left unattended or reacted to in an anxious, inappropriate or clumsy fashion, then the process of escalation to actual physical aggression is pushed forward.

Disruptive behaviour occurs when someone wants attention immediately.

Recognise instrumental aggression

One possible source of aggression is important to recognise at its outset, and is considered now before more driven sources of anger. Instrumental Aggression is when somebody uses violence or threats for his or her own deliberate purposes. It always shows as sudden disruption, and is often met by people at work who provide services of all kinds. With experience it is possible to discriminate quite quickly between genuine distress or anxiety aggression, and very deliberate or calculated acts – although both can present as a disruption. Instrumental aggression is usually for one of the following reasons:

- Criminal intent (i.e. demanding money with menaces).
- To get advantageous treatment (i.e. to be taken first in turn or given a privilege).
- To escape legitimate expectations or demands (i.e. pay a fine, or hand over 'contraband').
- To bully (i.e. a dysfunctional need to control or dominate others).

When aggression is clearly instrumental – and it always is with bullying – the response must be clear. In most situations this means to simply offer a cool explanation of your expectations and the consequences otherwise, set out in the context that it will be their choice for this if they continue; and a quick response if the behaviour continues. In many situations, it is perfectly appropriate to quietly continue with your work in hand after offering the choice. Certainly showing, or bowing to pressure, reinforces to the bully that their tactics work (they are tactics), and not placing responsibility very evidently squarely on the other person, as their choice, can cause the issue to gain ground and emotions to rise (yours and theirs), and all will worsen. Not everyone is this assertive, but instrumental aggression is usually clear to see because what the person is demanding is blatant. These deliberate acts must be recognised, resisted, and police involvement and criminal charges made use of when appropriate.

The chain to action

Genuine anger and how to act on it can be deconstructed; it is a thought chain. The chain may be processed through in seconds or a very much longer time period. When there is time and the chain of stages is recognised it can be interrupted by skilled intervention or responses appropriate to the given stage. The chain of stages is:

- Trigger or Event stage:
  Something causes arousal, and is at work on emotions. The person is just becoming stirred up (the brow furrows, or the person shows surprise). The reaction to the trigger (word or event) is instinctive and difficult to disguise. Minor disruption often begins here as a reaction (i.e. a verbalisation such as 'damm' or a fist is made, or a table thumped). At this point a strong distraction or quick enquiry can focus or redirect the person's attention and disrupt the chain.

- Appraisal or Thinking stage:
  Brain patterning occurs (the predictive model) and this matches the present view or experience of events to past experience and feelings. A unique personal view or mood comes quickly to the fore and becomes embedded into the current viewpoint (i.e. *'Here we go again – I'm never trusted!'*). This may be an habitual and dysfunctional cognitive connection, or quite realistic depending on the particular person and circumstances. At this point it can be helpful to ask what the person is thinking.

- Anger or Feeling stage:
  Once a strong feeling is identified it can be used to excuse a strong response. Giving vent to feelings is much more likely if the other person (you) mirrors their arousal, or gets involved in 'tit for tat' (a *'yes you did – no I did not'* repartee). By now a fair number of warning signals will be displayed (see below). External input at this stage can be inflammatory or calming depending on its nature. Quick intervention in a non-threatening manner can still calm emotions, particularly if it helps the feelings to be acknowledged verbally, and by altering the environment (removing to a quieter or different place – this might be more or less public, depending on the situation).

- Inhibition or Evaluation stage:
  A moment of reflection: what's stopping me? Personal moral values, or clear undesirable consequences will most often stop behaviour escalating (you show fear, security arrives, a warning notice makes impact, or the person does not want to become a public spectacle). Effective intervention at this stage reminds one of consequences, and directs the person towards alternative and more acceptable forms of expression – you help process the complaint or concern by accepting it.

- Active Aggression stage:
  Behaviour crosses normal boundaries and becomes acted out, verbally or physically or both, and with increasing intensity. Rational thought is now left behind and behaviour

becomes more instinctive, driven solely by the strong emotion or within an addictive pattern, and fuelled by an adrenaline charge. Intervention is not likely to be successful unless it carries considerable authority, personal control (i.e. favoured companion or relative) or is physically overpowering.

Unfortunately there is no common pace, and people can arrive at the active aggression stage within seconds, in which case intervention is more difficult. However, before people become physically aggressive they usually show their arousal with ritualised signals. The time to act or seek help is as the warning signals show. These are useful when recognised as they inform about the other person's level of arousal. But being aware of the warning signals serves two purposes – there are at least two people involved in any conflict, and observing self will also help alert you to your own level of stress-arousal. There are behaviour and physiological changes.

Behaviour changes

Changes in behaviour and manner are usually observable and include:

- Sudden change of voice level/manner – raised or very quiet, pointed articulation.
- Slow rise in voice pitch or level as arousal changes.
- Depersonalised language (you lot . . . people like you . . . this company is . . . or the person talks about themselves in the third person).
- Language becomes threatening, abusive, racist.
- Prolonged eye contact – staring.
- Raising eyes/turning head to look over or past the subject.
- Excessive or repeated activity (tapping, kicking, head nodding, fidgeting, pacing, walking faster, folding and unfolding documents).
- Faster breathing/exhaling loudly; smokers blow out hard.
- Head held back – jutting jaw.
- Drawing up to full height; standing from sitting.
- Exaggerated hand or arm gestures, pointing with finger.
- Closing-up normal interpersonal distance (usual western culture body space is just over a metre)
- Raising arms – taking hands from pockets or from around companions.
- Other abrupt stop or start behaviour, or returning to earlier behaviour (NB it can take 20–90 minutes to calm completely).

Physiological changes

Physiological changes are not all observable and most are not as readily apparent in others as self, but they include:

- rapid breathing – more oxygen needed
- flushing/blotching – sweating
- heart beats faster – blood pressure rises (ticking vein in neck)
- pupils may dilate
- tension of muscle tone
- sudden mental alertness
- dry mouth
- clenched teeth
- 'butterflies' in stomach
- feeling hot or sick
- blood clotting agents increase

Physiological changes are autonomic, and as they are spontaneous they are good indicators of the level of arousal. If these, and the behaviour markers increase or become stronger they will begin to merge into the danger signs that show the aggressor is about to lose control. However, it may be too late to take a commanding response or alternative action once danger signs occur. It will then be a matter of personal safety, and likely too late to defuse the other person or manoeuvre yourself into a less vulnerable position.

Danger signs

The significantly different and spontaneous behaviour that precedes actual attack includes:

- Pushing away, stabbing with finger or holding by the arm or collar.
- Face goes pale (blood away from extremities).
- Lowering the head (to protect throat).
- Lips tighten over teeth.
- Hooding the eyes (eyebrows drop to protect eyes).
- Shoulders tense up (for attack).
- Hands rise above waist.
- Stare is broken – the aggressor drops eyes to the area of your person they will grab or punch.
- Stance changes to side on (an instinctive move to protect the body and improve balance).
- Whole body lowers – especially if you are out of reach.

- They move forward.
- Move towards, or actual take up, of potential weapon (chair, instrument).

Context

Of the many situations that may increase the likelihood of conflict, the more common include:

- **Issue** – the person is making a complaint or a demand and especially if they repeat their words, or are asked to do so insensitively.
- **Frustration** – you block an exit, or try to detain someone; a person brings a complaint that has been made before, or you have to deny a request.
- **Imposition** – you have asked for compliance or made a request, threat, or demand, or worse, offered a 'do it or else' form of challenge.
  – Or another person with authority has presented an uncaring or dismissive attitude.
  – Or your task is to confront anti-social behaviour (e.g. probation officer).
- **Transference** or **Contagion** – others around the person are angry or have been complaining.
- **Agent** – a third person has been goading or stirring up trouble.
- **Self-esteem** – peer pressure so as not to lose face (age or culture related); and you may feel pressure not to lose face before colleagues, clients, or public.
- **Sleep deprivation** – late at night or early morning, jet lagged, other sleep loss.
- **Physical stimuli** – the person is too hot, or cold, thirsty, or in pain (e.g. hospital A and E).
- **Changes of order** – the other person is told of delay, cancellation, etc.
- **Substances** – effect of drink or drugs.
- **Life changes** – bereavement, loss of job, etc.
- **Environmental** – physical surroundings are squalid, noisy, or remote, or the social surroundings are tense, excited, hostile (e.g. a losing football crowd), or you are seen as an intruder into the other persons home or 'territory'.
- **Poor signalling** – you (or a colleague) use aggressive body posture or language, or show signs of anxiety, even if unintentional.
- **Cultural mismatching** – differences between what you and the other person think of as normal behaviour in the circumstances and this may be age, culture, or nationality differences.

Aggression is frequently not a strongly deliberate or premeditated stance, so much as **a form of distress**. Often a series of events can cause people to begin to see themselves as victims or suffering injustice. This feeling may be close to the outset of difficulties, but comparatively weak. It is then that subsequent events compound their view and very often do really worsen their problem – think of the stories that the media makes use of when consumers meet problems complaining about a product or service. With very bad situations or series of experiences people can feel as if they are losing control of part of their lives; with neither power over the circumstances that have brought them to the position they are in, nor of their consequent emotion.

Distressed persons may often be teetering on giving physical vent to their feelings (action or tears), but this vulnerability can also make them very open to a sympathetic approach and demonstrations of concern. Effective intervention means finding out what is the context and source of anger, and to seek a solution.

The CARMA© model for managing distressed persons

The Carma model provides a safe way to deal with anyone who is angry and aroused whoever they are. It is helpful to confidently tap into one's own empathy and remember an angry person is, in any event, a distressed person (even if very cross about something and looking for someone 'to pay for it'). They need their feelings to be discharged and may be desperate for their case to be heard, for a helpful response, some form of care, or for justice, or whatever is their need as they perceive it. This means helping the other person to process through a sequence of stages – and being prepared to return to an earlier stage if needs be. This process is in some ways similar to stages of grief – although much more rapid, and it can include denial (oh no! not me!), and anger, through to acceptance or new action.

No matter in what way you might be confronted, before you engage the other person it is essential to make some rapid decisions:

You must first decide and act in this order:

- *You leave* (the situation looks altogether too alarming).
- *You need help* (aware that you must not leave this until too late).
- *You stay* (and are willing to give time and attention to conclusion).

Use the mnemonic **CARMA** to guide your professional response; copy it down where it will be of use to you as an aid to memory.

CARMA

Calm ▶ Relate ▶ Manage

Calm

- *Listen* if staying – this is calming.
- *Encourage* them to tell their story.
  - Do not make evaluative comment.

Relate

- *Exchange names.*
  - Give your first name – avoid status, or making them feel inferior.
- *Understand* (facts).
- *Empathise* (feelings).
- *Check out detail.*
- *Concentrate:* show the other person you care.
  - Ignore the phone/others, move away from distraction.
- *Watch the other's body language*: gauge response.
- *Watch your body language.*
  - Do not crowd.

Manage

- *Clarify anything not understood.*
  - *Sit beside* – possibly go somewhere quieter or more comfortable.
- *Work out with them what is best to do.*
  - *Prioritise what you are doing* – do not pass the person on.
- *Determine an action plan.*
  - *Clarify* their concern.
  - *Order* the priorities.
  - *Be honest* about what you will do.
  - *Advise* further.
- *Review* the situation.
- *Write down important points (dates/details/action).*
- *Satisfy* the other person.

Managing anger is helped by preparation. Remember also to be aware of yourself and your needs, and after a disturbing event get 'karma' yourself. Coping with very aggressive behaviour is demanding, and you may have been frightened, and be left feeling shaky and exhausted.

There is a powerful psychological process at work when angry or distressed persons are helped to voice their problem. It is akin to the process used in counselling. When the person makes their distress public – even if only to you – it is externalised. This is already therapeutic; the distress is now 'out'; it exists, and can be dealt with. Next, when you rephrase or paraphrase the problem, you will give it better or more formal existence, particularly as you will likely have better words to describe the feelings or the problem the person has. This also strongly confirms the problem as a reality. Denying problems, or rejecting the feelings of others, is a huge cause of anger. Now the problem is part owned by you; and so the process alters perception from lone anger into shared solution.

Remember with CARMA the first thing is to decide to stay or not. The best way to prevent injury to you is to leave. Purposefully walk away. It may be better to get others or the police to deal with the situation.

If one is trapped, or frozen, a non-confrontational response does not usually worsen the situation, and some reasonable reactions can assist personal safety. A natural response to threatened violence is to drop to a semi-crouch and/or raise hands to protect head or throat. This is quite an arresting sight, and if your would-be assailant is separated from you by a moment or two of distance, the chances are that their higher order thinking will have time to work sufficiently to stop the attack being driven home. This is especially so if you have no emotional connection with the assailant, or do not represent oppression and the physical threat and intimidation will reduce to words.

Professional response

Expectations of professional response

In any interpersonal conflict a professional person is reasonably expected to exert some professional self-discipline and appropriate skills. Professional expertise is based on choosing one's own behaviour, and not being reactive or panicked. This requires constant self-awareness even during an event that might otherwise create considerable emotion. Confident thinking ahead ensures confrontational exchanges do not have harmful outcomes.

Training helps proper professional responses, and actual confrontation will test if the following **personal and organisational attributes** are in place or done, as appropriate:

- You acted confidently and are self-aware.
- You assessed the environment, the state of self and the other person before you decided how best to proceed.
- You acted before a situation deteriorated out of your control; and you determined what you think the best response or action (competency is as much established by forethought as efficacy – even if difficulties worsened, it is important to be able to show that you thought your actions through).
- You assessed personal risk, and any threat to others.
- You gave thought and assessed any further risks as the event unfurled.
- You were consistent – you were clear about the stance or attitude of your organisation, and you remained politely firm.
- You deliberated forward – you posited possible outcomes not as threat, but as choice (good and bad consequences) for the aggressor to consider.

- You acted upon past planning and training for a safe environment.
- You drew upon training that provided an array of skills and techniques.
- You were confident appropriate help and support was in place, and you were mindful of the clear policy and procedure for dealing with the event and you kept to this (see Chapter 6 on Health and Safety).
- You were solution seeking – you sought a win-win path out of the situation.
- You know proper resolution will help reduce this kind of event reoccurring – the aggressor learns that there are no gains to be got from using bullying or confrontational tactics.
- You and your organisation are able to learn from undesirable events and take the best measures you can to preclude repeat.

Confrontations are worsened by reactive responses. Reactive responses can be quite varied, but common causes are anxiety, or an inappropriate need for instant dominance or control. This will show by actions such as shouting back, making pompous repartee, or counter-threat.

Reactive responses usually:

- Lack consideration – may show panic.
- Are inconsistent – your stance may shift rapidly from alarm to threat.
- Tend to have other problem outcomes – loss of mutual respect, loss of self-respect, other unpredicted results (a walkout, some form of physical or mental collapse).
- Are inflammatory – likely to increase the intensity of aggression and result in physical action by one or both parties.
- Are power driven solutions – your desire to 'win' this actual confrontation because you see self as a higher status individual?
- Can extend the particular conflict – both parties vie for dominance – the classic 'slanging match'.
- Increase the likelihood of repeat event – there will be a standoff, and the outcome will be resolved on another occasion; or you win they lose, and they will return later for a chance to even the score; or they win you lose, and you will be seen as an easy rollover for any repeat confrontation.

People otherwise quite ordinary, but with reason to be angry, will differ in the degree and manner of their reaction to situations; however very distressed persons, and those with interpersonal, social, or behavioural problems will be more extreme in their presentation. They, like you or I, will differ in the degree and manner of their reaction, only their aggressive responses are probably already symptomatic of their condition, and coupled with inappropriate expectation, greater frustration, or difficulty understanding (cognitive misinterpretation). Their response will be stronger or more readily aroused, and although the trigger to violence may seem obvious, the real source of that feeling can be obscure. Whatever the situation, behaviour met with hostility or controlled out of expression is not therapeutic, nor the way to find a solution. The trick is to find the balance between care and control.

Presenting self in a positive and assertive manner is the essential beginning. It provides a role model – it demonstrates the actions, stance, and language of a person with secure self-worth. This can be done with an empathetic manner and without the need to alienate the other person; and it will protect you from attack and will help make the other person feel secure with you.

However, not all open-handed approaches receive a positive response. Sometimes people are too aroused to 'hear' sensitive responses; and sometimes when situations do not improve, your own anger may build up. Eventually you might overreact. Or contained, your anger will add to your stress.

Self-observation

Being aware of your own level of arousal is critically important, as this will influence the emotional state of the other person (see 'Warning Signals' above). The signals that emanate from you can calm or inflame the situation. Unless you are able to remain sufficiently cool headed and monitor your own body and verbal language, your signals are likely to result from instinctive autonomous reactions and state of own arousal.

The expression, 'take a deep breath and plunge in', has some substance. The best way to overcome a physiological reaction and so ensure control of self is by releasing tension in the stomach muscles. Take a deep breath through the mouth, hold it for two or three full seconds to oxygenate your blood before letting it slowly out. This also can give you a moment for thought, because plunging in may not always be wise.

The professional person will realise when caught off guard they are more likely to act or speak without proper thought. They will seek to control and monitor their internal processes, as dealing with difficult people will risk their own behaviour boundaries to be passed, or they might project reactive anger or a defensive attitude that makes the aggressor even more violent in response. Good or bad signals will emanate from instinctive self-presentation and current mood unless counteracted by self-awareness and personal control. They must seem calm on the surface, even if 'paddling desperately underneath'. The main things to watch are:

- Face
    - Face the other person – show concern and concentration.
    - Tilting head to one side indicates the listening stance.

- Keep a natural eye contact as if in normal conversation. If the other person is making you uncomfortable by staring, look at them centre forehead between the eyes (avoid flicking your gaze from eye to eye as this can seem nervous).
- If other interruption, or excuse for thought comes to hand (you need to consult paper work or someone else, etc.), say 'excuse me a second'.

- Tone and pitch of voice
  - Anxiety can involuntarily raise voice pitch and loudness – sometimes the initial response is a strangled squeak.
  - Keep voice low and even.
  - Avoid authoritative overtones (which can come across as challenging, or patronising).

- Posture
  - Do not make sudden movements or postural change. You may feel more comfortable and safer standing than sitting, if so, do this casually, and ideally before any exchange worsens.
  - Keep hands and arms relaxed and by your side.
  - Do not fold arms.
  - Do not take up a posture that tenses your muscles.

- Hand gestures
  - Avoid anything that may be misinterpreted as a threat (i.e. pointing).
  - Do not raise hands or arms or make sudden gestures.
  - Keep hands open, palms to the other person.

- Proximity
  - Keep a comfortable (and safe) distance (normally a metre or more – 3–4 foot in western society).
  - Do not crowd the other person; the need for personal body space increases in conflict.
  - If you are crowded, avoid backing away suddenly as this space may well be encroached upon, thus backing you into a corner. Use the 'waddle back' technique of short slow steps back rocking a little from side to side.

Long term hazards

In tense environments with constant confrontation to personal safety and calm, the long-term stress this brings will have outcomes. Emotions may be contained differently because you have learnt, or do not allow, your reactions to be reasonably normal. Other concerns may cause you to be non-assertive, or feelings to be kept rigidly contained for fear of loss of self-control. Typical settings are when everyone is physically captive in some repeated way. Examples include in classrooms, in prison wings or work groups, at meal times, and some forms of reception work. These circumstances can produce one or more of the common physical or psychological symptoms of long-term stress whether they are very routine or more exceptional events:

- Cardiovascular: pounding heart, hypertension, sweats.
- Respiratory: asthma attack, squeaky voice, or hyperventilation.
- Muscular: backache, headaches, hand tremor, tension aches in shoulder and neck.
- Immune system: tonsillitis, colds, skin and hair problems, arthritis, allergies.
- Gastric or metabolic: bowel pain or difficulty, change of appetite.
- Psychological: cravings for food or sex, increase in consumption of alcohol or tobacco or other substances, sleeping difficulty, mood change.

Firm positive assertion is not always easy to achieve without the support of colleagues and an affirmative work culture. If a person is unable to address their feelings, or supervision does not give space for this, anger can slowly build up. This anger held may eventually be released with an overreaction, but this will likely cause attendant problems to follow.

One way to develop more assertive responses is to safely release some anger **while you are still in control**. This will assist you to be psychologically and physically healthier, and help preclude actual loss of self-control. This is not the same thing as taking out feelings on a pillow, punch bag, or the cat! That is 'rehearsal'. It is sometimes advised to angry young people that they should 'take out their feelings' on something inanimate. However, this is ill-advised as it allows the feelings to be linked to action (punching or kicking) that may well be actually enacted, rather than linked to methods of inner control or sublimation.

It is perfectly appropriate in some instances to chastise, or be cross. It is very possible and very useful to tap into your feelings and give the other person a tirade. There is the famous account of Khrushchev table thumping with his shoe to make his point at a world summit, except he had gone to the meeting with an extra shoe for table thumping!

A useful trick is to play-act your anger.

Play-acting helps keep the real physiological responses some way ahead, and to be angry as a decided response before you might become angry as a reaction. Although this is not possible for all situations, it can often be used, and it is a good tool to add to your repertoire of skills. It presents the person in your charge with secure and clear boundaries, and represents an honest outcome of their behaviour on you.

Play-acting anger in a safe situation can be a particularly useful training exercise. How to avoid going the whole distance is a professional skill – it needs to be practiced. This kind of training is much the same as that included in programmes aimed at helping people to become more self-assertive, and usually includes different scenarios when participants in turn take role-play and observation.

In the real work situation, because you are part of the dynamic in an encounter, your overt and subliminal communications are part of a two way process. How you respond, and what you do, can make the situation better or worse. Invariably a substantial loss of your control will cause the situation to deteriorate rapidly. The other aroused person will already be subliminally alert to all the clues you are giving out.

Self-control, self-observation, and self-awareness are crucial for the successful handling of aggressive feelings – yours as well as others'.

The techniques

Professional persons normally have an array of skills or techniques to draw upon, and will determine what to use in each situation. In this context the main techniques presented (Chapters 1–5) have been well tried and are in use in one form or another in lots of different settings, and all will help reduce the potential for conflict. You may recognise some or have a different name for a particular intervention. A number of these techniques have been developed from the work of Fritz Redl with delinquent youth in America of the 1950s. He was keen to identify means to reduce the disruptive behaviour that got in the way of more therapeutic experiences.

The techniques may not always be mutually compatible. Situations and people can so differ that there are no techniques that can be viewed as 'one size fits all'. One may seem to contradict another. You will need to be selective according to the situation you are in, and how well the technique suits your way of working, or is useable within your workplace. It is a proper area of professional decision making to determine appropriate new techniques within normal operational methodology, whether this is for you alone or for a team of people. Weigh up each situation and decide on your response, but remember:

- Aggression is a reaction to something that has already happened.
- Disruption is usually the first level of aggression and is the point for intervention.
- A professional person makes a considered response.
- A professional response ensures everyone's personal safety.

The professional in a situation: activity one

Allow about thirty minutes for this activity, a little longer if more than one person is involved.

This situation is deliberately not tightly context tied. It may help to flesh out the situation by basing your imagination on a place, a setting, or a person you have known in some small way.

Sue and Barney

Sue has just started a discussion session with a small group of young adults with learning and behavioural difficulties. This is part of a social skills training programme. The room she has to use is a bit too small for the six or seven people she has. Some tables are pushed back and the chairs are arranged in a rough circle. Sue is keen for the sessions to go well as there is someone who has really begun to benefit, and she feels she needs tangible progress for her contract to be renewed at the end of the year.

Suddenly Barney barges in, he is the only one who is late, and is grumbling about something. He immediately trips, treading on somebody's feet, and a slanging match breaks out. Sue stands up, approaches Barney and moderately chastises him, whereupon Barney turns his cussing onto her and spits at her. Sue nimbly avoids the spit, but responds angrily, and even shouts. Sue remains standing in front of Barney and puts her arms on her hips. She harangues him crossly for a moment or two, about the way he came in and for spitting at her. Sue puts out an arm intending to direct Barney to a chair . . .

Consider fully the dynamics, and what may have a bearing on the interaction. Make a set of conclusions to account for:

● What thoughts or observations you have, or what theory may be relevant?

● What possible consequences to Sue and Barney can you imagine?

Make **two** sets of notes or lists:

1. Outcomes with the scenario as given.

2. How Sue could have responded differently, and what are possible alternative outcomes.

After the activity

Did you reason that it would be all right for Sue to be angry? If so, she may be reacting and has dropped her professional guard and become a 'regular' person. It may be OK, it may be her anger is under control and is something she wants Barney to learn to deal with. But if Sue has lost control, she has placed herself on an equal footing with Barney. Now there are two aggressors. Both of them are bristling and alarmed. This is a situation with potential for disaster.

Of course Barney may acquiesce. Sue has authority behind her and Barney may have sufficient control to be afraid of later consequences. But the session may well be spoilt by difficulties continuing with Barney, or Sue, with her lost composure, may direct things poorly. Both Sue and Barney will have a bad experience of each other.

Perhaps Barney may misinterpret what Sue intends with her arm and strikes out. What Barney and Sue both might seem to be experiencing is a heady cocktail of misdirected anguish, frustration, and anger. This then is not a moment of supportive contact, but of conflict.

A set of notes is given for comparison and they may be especially useful if you did not do this activity with colleagues. The notes are by no means exhaustive. In a way this reflects work with people, in that what the potentials are, and what may be relevant, are not easily bounded. Because of this no attempt is made to itemise key factors, as the actual circumstances in any one setting are so variable.

The point of an exercise like this is to recognise the range of relevant possibilities and as such it is intended to broaden perspective rather than suggest absolutes. There is no score, just compare the type and range of what you have produced to the lists given and consider where there has been congruency or diversion of thought processes, and perhaps why. Remember there are no right or wrong answers. There are only issues. These, for example, may be to do with the type of setting, and its treatment model, with Sue's confidence, experience and training, or with tensions that may exist for Sue or Barney.

These are the kind of issues that have a bearing on responding to aggression, and I hope to demonstrate that a response can antagonise or resolve. Individual professional response is seldom fully isolated from its setting. The issues associated with items in the lists all relate to the content of this book, and if you return to this activity at the end of reading it, it may be interesting for you to see if your skill base, insight, and depth of vision has expanded. Each list is not presented in any special order, although items could be grouped into varied subsets.

- Sue's body language, words, and actions show anxiety and Barney becomes anxious/ aggressive.

- Barney desperately needs external control and constantly provokes responses that will provide the security he wants. Sue has not been appraised of this or does not recognise or know it.

- Barney does not trust Sue to contain him. (His outbursts in her presence may continue to escalate until some resolution is achieved.)

- Sue may be overreacting to Barney as she is too anxious about her need for success.

- Sue is more concerned about the group member who is progressing, or about her contract, than about Barney, and he knows she has little interest in him.

- Barney misinterprets Sue's intentions and he strikes out. Sue is injured/not injured. Problems ensue. Her supervisors question her suitability. Sue questions her suitability. Sue and Barney remain wary of each other.

- Barney realises he has gone too far. He knows he will be in trouble and other staff will back Sue up. He will be in for a hard time if he does not quickly settle down. (The establishment always supports staff if they are in conflict with residents/clients.)

- Other group members get involved in the fracas.
- Why has Barney come in already upset? Why is he late? Should Barney's problem have been attended to before the session? What support is Sue getting from colleagues?
- How was the group composition arrived at? Should Barney be there? Does he want to be there? Is he made to go – if so by whom, and why?
- What are the criteria for the renewal of Sue's contract? Why does she feel she needs 'tangible success'?
- Is Sue working in a situation that stretches/is beyond her ability?
- What supervision does Sue receive? (Is she struggling to do her best in difficult circumstances?)
- Sue is new to this group, should she be involved in the dynamics of group work (even if expert) without some support from workers who know the individuals better? (Is there a culture of everyone surviving for themselves?)
- Sue is new: her presence and the sessions are a departure from the group's past experience, and so are threatening/anxiety provoking. (Barney is the most vulnerable member, but Sue does not know this.)
- Barney was tripped – was this deliberate? What parts do other group members play?
- What are Sue's guidelines – should the spitting have been a signal for her to summon help?
- Sue responded to Barney at the outset, and her first words are chastisement (negative reinforcement), she did not ignore his manner of entry nor his mood. Barney has been a nuisance to her before (her condition takes precedence over any therapeutic or behaviour theory that should encompass Barney).
- What model of intervention/therapy informs Sue's actions, and informs her planned group work?
- Sue does not like/is afraid of Barney. Her reaction is a half recognised wish/intention/provocation that he is removed from the group.
- Barney is infatuated with Sue and does not know how to deal with it.
- Barney wants Sue's attention – this kind of outburst has got him attention in the past.
- Barney does not like Sue/these sessions, and has deliberately set out to get a reaction, or be removed.

How Sue could have responded differently, and with what possible alternative outcomes?

- Sue ignores Barney and stays seated until he settles and she is supported by the rest of the group – it's called the 'we are waiting until we are all ready game' (Barney has put this to the test before).

- Sue immediately goes to Barney concerned that he is uncharacteristically upset: she soothingly voices her observation of his mood, and will not begin the session until Barney's upset is resolved. (It may be beneficial to Barney/others to involve other members of the group.)

- Sue has known a moment like this would occur, she has been working long enough with the group to know that they are now familiar enough with her to drop any guard they might otherwise have of strangers, but her therapeutic model rather jars with the establishment she is working in. She cannot rely on immediate or methodological support from outside the room. Sue tries to relax and she defuses Barney using humour and by cowardly rounding on the person whose feet had sparked the incident, but she is resolved that she can no longer ignore the situation she is working in, and if she is to continue, a number of issues to do with support, methodology, and objectives must be better resolved.

- Sue is surprised and initially angry at Barney for his disruption, she is unsure of how to proceed, but she draws on her training, quickly realising she must not respond in a way that makes him worse, she sits back down and begins to monitor herself and her interventions with Barney.

- Sue often works with artificial or stale problems with this group – here is a live example relating to social skill, and she rejoices at something immediate to deal with. Her notes will help demonstrate the worth of her work at review time.

- Sue is concerned for Barney who has low self-esteem and seldom manages a day without some confrontation. She really feels for him, and does not want to reinforce his self-perceptions of being someone always in conflict, and Sue responds accordingly.

- Sue is pleased to see this outburst: she works within a therapeutic model that welcomes an open expression of anger as a healthy development for Barney (previously repressed or expressed deviantly).

- Sue is quiet but firm and tells Barney what she expects. She will summon help or ask Barney to leave if he does not settle. (This is a predetermined strategy for any group member including Barney, for dealing with disruption – the establishment works quite clinically within clearly defined terms.)

- Sue is firmly confrontational with Barney until he settles. (Anger management may be an issue for Barney and may be part of what her group work is about. Importantly, Sue is confident because she knows if the situation escalates she can quickly call for support, but all goes well.) Later Sue is able to compliment Barney on how well he managed to put aside his mood and settle (building up self-perceptions as able to self-control), and she asks if she can help with his upset.

- Sue tells both parties to quit their slanging match, she leaves the room and asks Barney to follow – she has reasoned it will be better to resolve any issue Barney has away from the audience (and the incitement) that the rest of the group would provide.

The event and its issues involve both Sue and Barney, and this reflects the reality of all conflict in that all those involved contribute to the dynamics of a situation.

Chapter 2

Interpersonal Immediate Techniques

This first group of ten techniques concerns responses in person-to-person situations that can be made fairly immediately in a variety of situations. The techniques are generally non-confrontational. They mainly affect surface behaviour, and the skills are very useful for managing a wide range of difficult client behaviours.

Ignoring (1)

Ignoring behaviour will render it ineffective and it will reduce until it stops (the psychological term is extinction of behaviour).

Simply to ignore behaviour will invariably lead to it dwindling away. Don't let it get to you by carefully manoeuvring around it. For example, making an issue of deliberate drumming on a table could make the drummer do it more often or loudly especially because he finds it annoys you, or gets him attention. A response that increases the tension in a situation will only make it worse, conflict become more likely. Always your original purpose is certain to be disrupted, so it is better not to wind up the behaviour by any focus on it. Do not see or hear it, in that sometimes it can be very useful to have a temporary affliction oneself.

Technically within the science of behaviour modification this is avoiding reinforcement. Response of any kind may act as turning a key to keep the behaviour going. Ideally, couple ignoring with a focus of attention on another behaviour that can be praised or given positive response. This is positive reinforcement. The technique is also valuable when applied to a series of events as part of a response to inappropriate and pestering demands. It is invariably safer to avoid conflict by making an alternative comment or by diverting attention (see Signals overleaf), than to challenge the form of disruption.

The triggers for all sorts of satisfactions can lie in the mechanism illustrated. This also has a bearing on the dynamics of physical and sexual abuse. Make sure you do not compound the problem. A person can be kept trapped into only coping with his feelings using violent outbursts. The cycle may have become addictive with 'pay-offs' at all the stages.

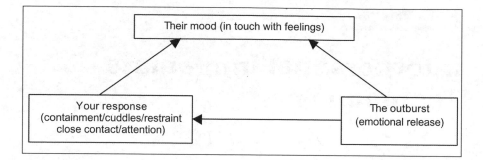

Reinforcement is obtained by giving either positive or negative attention. Sometimes it seems the two can get muddled. Take the case of a child who wants attention from a favoured member of staff, but finds it easier to get it by being naughty and receiving punishment. Maybe the worker is invariably too busy or is 'better' at responding to bad behaviours. Step back and see if inappropriate behaviours may have their origins in a need for attention.

Other needs must not be ignored, nor your own needs. If the technique does not seem to have enough effect, and you continue to put up with something that really is intolerable to you, then you are doing both yourself and 'the drummer' a disservice. Sometimes putting up with the stress of constant disruption, or of threatening behaviour is not the best course. Personally, it may be too costly, or it may not show the aggressor when their behaviour is unacceptable.

Conversely, the other person might not know how to communicate in a proper manner; perhaps they do not have the social skills to initiate proper assistance. Disruption and aggression may be a way to communicate.

> Gaz was a boy of 11 years, small and foul mouthed with repellent ways. He had been to many children's homes. One of his tricks was to pummel his care workers like a boxer at his punch bag. This caused them to retreat and make complaints, until one day Marissa began to respond by taking him in a bear hug and pulling him to her. He resisted on each occasion, but his resistance became less and less. Eventually one day he asked Marissa for a cuddle.

A client may lack confidence to approach a difficult subject, be anxious and uncertain about some procedure, or experienced rejection in the past when using milder behaviour. Starting out with some aggression can make it easier to cope with expectations of rejection, and allows for the projection outwards of feelings of inadequacy. Some clients will have learnt that this is a way of getting attention to their problems. Similar behaviour in the past has probably led to the resolution of a problem because there had been a sensitive response from other professionals, but not accompanied by learning better ways to communicate.

Often a legitimate request or plea lies behind aggressive ways of seeking a hearing. For example, if somebody keeps pestering with petty problems they may be trying to determine the receptivity of the person concerned, and building up courage to approach the problem they really have. This scenario may be taken analogously for other situations. If disruptions are frequent ask yourself what may be causing them, and how you are to determine what that is. Even if it is essential that you cope with the difficult behaviour immediately, and find that ignoring causes it to reduce, there may be a genuine difficulty that needs expression. It is always worth finding a way of approaching the other person later.

The technique is one of the most powerful as an agent for changing behaviour and has a long history of researched application that began with the work of behavioural scientists such as Skinner and Pavlov. It is also important to understand the process of this technique, because ironically it can attract attention from others if they are scrutinising your work. Ignoring behaviour can attract criticism when it is not understood or supported.

One feature in the pattern of behaviour before it is 'extinguished' is that it will often peak in intensity just prior to it stopping. This may be the moment when you come under most pressure for direct intervention. Be prepared for challenge from colleagues and managers. You may need to find some support in addition to your own persuasive skills to pave your way, as in some settings the technique may be too novel or not acceptable, and you may be seen as weak or even subversive.

Ignoring threatening or disruptive behaviour can cause it to reduce to the point of stopping. The behaviour may be an inadequate way of seeking attention.

Proximity and touch control (2)

Use physical proximity or a light touch to exert control over others.

Generally this will be an intervention rather than a counter to mounting aggression directed at you, but not uniquely so. It can be very disarming to respond to a verbal attack by a quick and non-threatening approach, such as perhaps to go and sit **beside** the person and show genuine concern that they are angry with you.

Proximity is about reducing personal space. A close body simulates a maternal form of relationship commonly associated between a mother and her child at a non-verbal developmental stage. This is when the infant is still closely attached to its parent as a source of security expressed through touch and comfort, and when the loss of such physical proximity raises anxiety and distress in the infant. The parental embrace is non-conditional. Use of the technique should reflect this emotional concern as much as possible rather than be a threatening move, particularly when responding to children or adolescents with arrested emotional development.

Body positioning

It is important whenever possible to place yourself **beside** the other person. This of course makes you more difficult to hurt, but there are other important considerations. Being beside a person is analogous with empathy – we speak of 'standing beside' others. It is not so easy to be emphatic or to gently challenge comments or assumptions when stood or sat more confrontationally positioned across from the other person. If the other person (or you) is upset or distressed enough to bring tears to eyes it can be easier to deal with when at one side (to pretend as unseen), and continue with the discussion, or maintain a focused professional approach.

This can be particularly important in instances that should include your consideration for gender or ethnicity. Many males will find it difficult to 'show' tears, and will deal with this by returning to aggressive feelings; and some cultures see eye contact as confrontational or inappropriate (particular examples in the context of male staff are some black males, and some Muslim girls); and generally many people (younger or older) will be uncomfortable with unfamiliar others seeing the degree of their distress.

A confrontation also needs a bit of actual space across which invective, objects, or the self can be hurled. The first level of proximity is simply to stand nearby.

John, a newly qualified teacher was a mature entrant to the profession. He taught well, but tended to command from the front of the class. He had some difficulties controlling a class that contained several quite disruptive pupils. A consultant showed him how to be more effective in his control by being more mobile, and to unobtrusively stand beside disruptive pupils as an intervention, all the while continuing with the lesson.

Next, a light hand on the shoulder or arm can make the same message stronger and be a non-forceful means of restraining a provocative tongue or a rising temper. The technique is nothing more than a common human gesture often done instinctively. Its use should not raise issues related to the use of restraint. However, a restraint policy and training should include very low-key intervention of this kind, and refer to physical proximity and touch as measures that may precede actual restraint.

Be wary that your proximity and manner do not cause you to become the target of the aggressor. It can be easy to take on an authoritative and threatening stance yourself, like a full frontal approach, with arms on hips or raised, and a tense angry voice. This sort of action may well provoke being punched, or worse. Far better, if you judge you need to hold the other person, is to sweep in to one side, firmly take an elbow, or put an arm around the shoulders and speak quietly.

Proximity is equally valuable in dealing with strangers. It can be better to relinquish the protection of an inquiry counter and by taking an elbow actually steer an angry complainant to a seat, all the while expressing your concern that something has so upset them. It is also not so easy for them to raise their anger when sitting. Conversely, to remain unmoved behind the counter and ask them to take a seat may provoke stronger reaction, as the counter could actually make it safer for them to work up more anger. Some agencies would do well to consider the implications of what they are signalling before erecting physical barriers.

Proximity has more potential for control than distance. Firstly, it signals you care or are concerned about the person, since you join their corner. Approach or a light touch are strong body messages. Proximity signals you are in control and confident, while backing away indicates uncertainty or anxiety. Secondly, you are now at hand. It is easier to restrain, if it comes to this, before a fully launched attack. Also with your body you can block the sight of an antagoniser and use your body as a screen, although beware that you are not hurt by something thrown from behind you.

At close quarters you do not need to shout, and keeping your voice calm and quiet not only allows you to resist your alarm mechanisms and the potential for generally raising the tension, but you can soothe and reassure with words heard only by your chosen ward. If with some choice inquiry, it is possible to deflect direct antagonism into an indirect complaint, the situation is becoming considerably de-escalated. Proximity also allows you to counter gestures or words of provocation from others, and it is easier now either to stroke, hold the person firmly, or steer them away.

In less certain situations, particularly if confronted by an angry stranger, beware. Although proximity means you may be safer from punches or thrown objects, you could be stabbed or gouged, or more easily grabbed as a hostage. Also, personal space enlarges as a person becomes angry. Enter this, or reduce the personal distance, and you may provoke the first physical contact as you are repelled, or attacked. It may be safer to step back a little. This space also gives the other person a little thinking time for their higher order thinking and inhibitions to occur.

In circumstances where there is high supervision and staffing ratios, 'body boxing' of an aggressor can be done with two or three people. When this is done with one either side and one shielding out of reach to the front, the person can be more easily and safely led away. Be aware, however, that with this degree of security the aggressor may now feel safe to give fuller vent to words or actions.

Proximity can be combined with other actions such as the 'wordy techniques' in Chapter Three. Echoing the complaint when appropriate is a powerful and morally just intervention. As a representative and person 'in charge', the complaint has now a more formal and depersonalised tone, a sort of registration of grievance, and your ward may not resist you easing them away from the situation. Repeating, using your own words, is called 'paraphrasing' and is a powerful technique used in counselling that allows feelings to be given shape, discharged and externalised.

Proximity can be effective management as a preventative measure. For example, when organising an outing it might be sensible to attach a member of staff to a particular individual such as the client that is provocative, bullying, or aggressive, or alternatively the client who is anxious, or who incites their own victimisation. This may also raise organisational issues to do with staffing levels and how to meet the needs of the client group, a consideration given later in the section on organisational health.

A note of caution. It is important to understand a psychological dynamic to do with the autonomy of persons. Stepping in to control every situation and you will exert authority, as an external and formal form of control. People who have poorly integrated components to their personality, or limited social skill may be denied chances to learn and progress.

Controlling may be sensible to avert a worse situation, but it does not help individuals to resolve conflict themselves unless some process of involvement is determined. Continual interruptive intervention without a programme for self-control will only debase a person further and lower their self-esteem. The client can become reliant on intervention, de-skilled, and without need of conscience. The client could come to believe that the blame for any hurt could also be yours for not intervening effectively, saying, perhaps, 'after all you know what I'm like when I'm cross'. When the locus of self-control and the locus for self-judgement remain in the hands of the controlling workers, it may be a peaceful place to work in, but only a more therapeutic approach will allow the slow and often painful progress towards autonomy.

Helping others manage feelings of anger is more effective if you are physically close to them.

Signals (3)

Establishing non-verbal forms of communication to assist control.

Making a contact is essential, and how you do this can set the tone for interpersonal reaction, however brief. This can make life a lot safer for you.

> Jane's work as community nurse took her to some tough inner city estates where she visited people at home. One worry she had was that she carried prescription drugs. Often she had to pass youths 'lurking with intent' (Jane's words) around the stairwells of tower blocks and flats. At first she felt very intimidated and would avoid eye contact, and she acted as if she expected to be a victim of their unwelcome attention.
>
> Following some assertiveness training Jane learnt to keep up a purposeful walk and use a smile, a passing remark, or some joke to give her the initiative in any contact. She has been scrounged for a smoke or two, but not mugged. More importantly she feels in control, and much less threatened from people once they have responded with a 'Hi' back to her. She has got to know one or two of the characters a little, and she feels less out of place.

No one likes to be ignored. The signal technique echoes body proximity in that it signals to the person that they or their actions are noticed. A useful way of avoiding giving offence or a reason for someone to vent their frustration or anger is to let them know you know they are there, and maintain some contact.

Imagine a visitor who arrives in a bad mood. You respond and perhaps get them to sit and wait, or you cannot actually attend or speak to them immediately. In this sort of situation a non-verbal dialogue can be a means for you to maintain contact. Secretly given raised eyebrows at some further delay signals 'I'm on your side'. Smile. Talk when and if you can, just do not ignore people. Ignoring them may trigger behaviour based on deeper experiences such as abandonment or rejection. Ignoring them can fuel whatever frustration, anxiety, or negative emotion they carry.

With an established relationship, tiny signals like a smile, frown, thumbs-up, touch, and a raised eyebrow, are all subtle but powerful forms of control. The signal interferes with the patterns of thought of the other person and reminds them you are minded about them. It is particularly useful in preventing behaviour deteriorating to the point of needing actual or direct intervention.

The use of signals is particularly useful to reinforce desired behaviour, of showing pleasure, and so supporting, at a distance, a desirable sequence of behaviours when the client is otherwise hesitant or anxious that they will fail in what they are doing. Signals are instantaneous. It is a good way of maintaining contact with individual clients within a larger group. It can become a form of secret two-way dialogue, and is something children particularly relish. It is also very useful when clients need support in public situations, and more direct intervention may be embarrassing or counterproductive.

The use of signal as interference simulates communication associated with a paternal relationship. Although still non-verbal it is based on a higher order of communication, and relates to the phase of child development when internalising externally imposed structure is beginning to occur. It is represented theoretically by the father's authority, and is a step on from maternal close body security, and the proximity technique. The communication is always related to a conditional situation, in that there is some judgement going on. Although the signal comes from someone else, as an external authority, it gives recognition and is a minimal intervention. It invites self-control and builds on internal loci (within the self) for self-appraisal and self-knowledge. Whether used to encourage or discourage, the common element in the signal is, 'I'm here, I'm watching, but I'm not actually going to . . .' Actual words can be used but these are not private or so personal, and often not as powerful.

Signalling lets the other person know they are in your thoughts and counters any feelings of isolation or being ignored. It can help others control frustration and manage their anger.

Involvement and interest (4)

Responding to disruption not by censure, but by diverting behaviour into positive outcomes.

Behaviour that is disruptive or designed to antagonise can often be diverted into something more constructive. This is especially useful with ego-disturbed children as it can build up the vitality of their interest fields, reduce the potential for guilt, or need of reparation, and be a way of building a relationship.

Fred was a Craft and Design teacher. He took on some new work with a group of young boys with emotional and behavioural difficulties. In one of his first sessions things were not going too well. He was already anxious when Johnny took a big T-square off the wall and made chopping motions with it. Fred asked him to put it back on the tool rack. Johnny was clearly intrigued with the tool, ignored Fred and struck the T-square on the bench, which can ruin the tool. Fred moved to take it from him, crying out, 'it's not an axe – silly boy'. He then suddenly found himself involved in a chasing game around the workbenches. All work stopped and the other boys began to look for 'weapons'. Fred rapidly lost his temper, he caught up with Johnny and, half in momentum and half in anger, slammed the child against the wall.

Another teacher may have been more skilled or experienced in this situation. Although the lesson may have started badly, it is also reasonable to view Johnny as a key figure in the group, and the boys are working without much interest or enthusiasm. When Johnny lifted down the T-square this may be seen as an opportunity. This would mean ignoring the banging, as any damage to the square has probably already happened, and to have dwelt on this would have added guilt to compound Johnny's feelings that probably included boredom and inadequacy (low self-esteem) in this workshop.

An alternative scenario might be as follows:

Fred looks up and addresses Johnny with interest:

> *Looks just like an axe, eh? Nice balance in your hands? Looks like just two bits of old wood joined up, eh? – but it's mega useful. Any ideas? What shape is this like?*

Fred has walked quietly up to Johnny (proximity) and runs his finger along the join of the instrument, but leaves it in Johnny's hands (non-confrontational).

> *Like a corner . . . square.*
>
> *Well done Johnny. That's exactly right, you've got the makings of a real workman* (ego-stroking). *I bet you can use it right first time* (diversion). *See this sheet of board . . . put the T-square up to the edge . . . look, like this . . .*

From this alternative scenario here is a list of the kind of desirable processes that it promotes:

- positive attention
- relationship building
- reinforces ego
- teaches skills
- promotes useful cognitive learning
- unconditional positive regard
- builds self-esteem
- offers positive self-construct
- sculpts behaviour (influence by suggestion)
- avoids conflict
- dismantles an undesirable role model
- offers a non-aggressive role model
- avoids disruption for the rest of the group
- maintains peer structures (but offers new basis)
- reduces the potential for damage to equipment, and possible client guilt

The example illustrates the treatment gains that can be got from interventions that are non-aggressive, and authoritarian only in that they offer to legitimise the behaviour in some way.

In the example, conflict was avoided and disruption diverted. Interest and involvement is of considerable use in managing anger away. Sometimes the anger of others is justified. In these instances the technique is an appropriate response to the other person. Offer thanks to them for a situation you can use to deal with the frustration that you share from your professional position. Divert their anger by supporting them into progressing their concern in a proper manner, and offer the correct routes for this. This can be a good way to attend to service limitations, and everyone wins.

Non-aggressive interested responses to others can divert or preclude their potential anger. It can divert behaviour into legitimate activity.

Injection of affection (5)

Greeting people with warmth will help disarm their anger, and protects you from their projected anger. The technique is multi-faceted.

Everyone benefits from support in the form of hugs, smiles and encouragements when they are unhappy or anxious. This is especially true at critical moments, and when attempting something difficult, and is especially so for people who lack personal or social skills.

Children with behavioural difficulties, in particular, try to ward off uncertainty about their self-worth by deliberately seeking reinforcement of their negative self-image. They will use an excuse for conflict to do this, or will present themselves in such a way as to invite rejection. Although these behaviours need to be dealt with, this is best done indirectly, and meeting and greeting others with acceptance sets up the best conditions for this.

Warm greetings are particularly valuable if your work routinely brings you into contact with people who may be aggressive, and when you work regularly with individuals who are known to have aggressive tendencies. It is a good idea to make contacts when coming on duty. Smile, say hello to everyone. This pre-empts hostile or aggressive attack, and reduces the trap of responding to a challenge by instant limitation or counter-threat. In a holding situation show your face to people who have come in while you have been off-shift by giving eye contact. At a hostel say hello to new people off the streets. Check that they are OK. *You will become an individual and less vulnerable to attack.* Strangers will feel that little more cared for and you will have given them an opportunity to air any worry.

Initiating contact echoes the strength and warmth of character implicit in the previous two techniques. This is about knowing the clients who need affirmations, and being sure they get the regular squeeze of approval and love, each day or hour, whatever the need is.

It also gives you a way of responding to anxieties you may have about the attitude of people you have to face. When you take the initiative you reduce your uncertainties and you can better evaluate, and influence, the mood of the other person. The chances are greater that a friendly welcome is reciprocated. Conversely, of course, the other person can have their prejudices and fears confirmed when they are ignored, or greeted coldly, or with obvious anxiety.

Affection has to include you. Managing aggression is stressful work. Watch out that you do not exhaust your emotional battery during the day, and look to see that you, and those in your private life, have their share of your positive approach. Take a moment occasionally to check that you have the emotion to spare to respond to them, as you would wish. Reward yourself with a treat from time to time.

Being sensitive to the moments of need in others may not change circumstances for them, but at that point 'an injection of affection' will help, and they will note you as a friend.

> I once worked with Kate, a residential social worker. She seemed to lighten up the place the moment she came on shift. Kate had a smile or comment for everyone she met, staff included. She was big, not at all self-effacing, and she carried a lot of personal pain; but it was difficult to feel morose or lonely in her company simply because of the very direct and accepting way she acknowledged the presence of people around her, including me. Kate became one of my most respected and cherished of colleagues.

Responding to others with personal warmth when greeting them, and at problem points, is effective in averting possible aggression.

Humour (6)

Tension-decontamination can diffuse much aggression.

Most people find it is impossible to laugh and be angry at the same time. Humour can be used rather like a shield. It will deflect the first blow, and allow you a moment of deeper thought. The tactic can surprise, and cause the aggressor to hesitate.

Jackie worked for a public utility. She manned a reception desk. Her customer service training had emphasised the importance of being calm and even-tempered, but she was feisty with a good sense of fun. On one occasion she was distracted by documents when a man surprised her. He suddenly appeared before her, and thumped hard upon her counter.

This caused Jackie to jump, but her instant response was to say: 'OK, OK, Buster. Waddya want de wimin or de money?'

The man was surprised in turn, and, after a second of hesitation he relaxed, laughed and apologised. Both shared the joke but she was then quick to point out he must be very annoyed and asked what she could do to help. Jackie was now in control of the encounter, and the man was then able to put his complaint properly to her. Her spontaneous tactic had surprised the complainant into a moment of uncertainty. This worked because it matched Jackie's personality and was balanced by her concern. Had she been stonewalled, Jackie said she would have got composed and been po-faced serious, but she would not be intimidated.

When an aggressor is 'disarmed' there is less tension in the situation. The use of humour can create a time space to allow the aggressor to momentarily review and discard their original stance and the emotion that supported it. It is better to laugh than to cry. The use of humour is usually most relevant in environments where people know each other well enough for the humorous response not to offend and create worse problems.

An issue presented in an aggressive manner by a client is sometimes taken up on their behalf in the same manner. Their aggressive stance is echoed by the professional. Perhaps the sense of injustice is shared (not as suggested in 'Involvement and Interest', above), for example, when communications have broken down, or another service provider has failed to get resources in the right place at the right time. Anger can be effective in getting a response from others. When this aligns the professional with the client, it is a cheap form of empathy, and saves them from further personal threat. However it will reinforce the use of aggression as means to ends.

It can sometimes work well with some clients to reflect their scenarios back to them (perhaps with a bit of ham acting) as a catalogue of comic disaster and tragedy – a form of neuro-linguistic programming. Using humour to process the problem offers an alternative set of constructs in which to couch the circumstances, and suggests a new way to behave.

Raw, and often constant aggressive behaviour is expressed by young people in difficulties. One way to respond humorously to hostile behaviour in teenagers is to surprise them by reflecting their behaviour (called mirroring, and a therapeutic technique in its own right, but in this example, the humour is the key facet).

Imagine a residential care setting, and a TV lounge in which there is some conflict about seating because there is a 'best chair'. A young person comes in and swears because 'their' chair is occupied, and because of their intimidation the chair is surrendered by a submissive peer. An adult supervising might decide to challenge this behaviour.

However, not only could challenge easily turn to confrontation, other TV viewers might object to interruption of their viewing by a conflict started by an adult, as they see it, and also the pecking order might be supported by them. An alternative response is to mirror the intimidation. This might be especially effective from a normally mild mannered adult, probably actually seated on the floor or the worst chair, who does as follows: they rise a moment or two later, and melodramatically look menacingly around, and perhaps with some swearing, make a comment such as, 'no-one had better nick my special chair while I'm gone', before stalking out. The seating could also be reviewed and the chair removed (see Chapter 5, Control of Environment).

Use humour to take the tension out of situations.

Appeal (7)

Reduce the intensity of the aggressor by reminding them that you are also a person who has needs.

Confrontational behaviour can be countered by an appeal to the aggressor for them to consider your needs. You must recognise the controlling power of the other person by acknowledging the fact that they are angry and they have an issue to deal with, but then you ask them for respite from their temper. Initially you neither promise action nor refuse it. Point out that you now have their anger as an issue for you to deal with. This will place you on an even footing with them, but your response is not to reflect the anger back. Instead you appeal to their goodwill.

This relates to the theory of transactional analysis (Harris, 1995) and represents a simple 'you and I' message that signals a status of equality with the other person. An even balance of power is maintained by your refusal to be subservient and give in to the aggression, but neither do you seek dominance by counter threat.

This is more useful when working with adults than young people, and particularly appropriate with people you know. You draw on their goodwill, and there may well be a fund generated from past good experiences. When their response is positive it allows you to thank or praise them later for their consideration, and so build up their positive self-perception.

Appeals can differ, depending on the circumstances. It may be appropriate to say you wish to complete your current task before you respond. Explain that you will have a problem as well if your work is not properly done. A client who impatiently demands attention may well respond positively if you tell them how tired or busy you are, and you ask that they please help by curtailing their immediate call on you. It can help to exaggerate the situation you are in. One way of doing this is to feign a difficulty.

> Bill was confronted in a hallway by an angry complainant whose voice and temper began to rise. Bill stepped back, rubbed his ear and interrupted. He explained he had trouble hearing just then following an infection, and the hall was too echoing for him, but he wanted to help. Bill managed to move to another room, which was safer as colleagues were nearer. He also gained time to think.

Counter anger in others and resist power imbalances by appeal.

Saying 'No' (8)

How a refusal is made will carry undertones that reveal self-confidence and personal authority.

Sometimes all a confrontational challenge needs is an authoritative response, and in the face of this the aggressive behaviour subsides. Often people just need some strong external control of the feelings sweeping them along. However, when a refusal or a denial is made, to be effective it must be made with confidence, and it must be backed up by follow through action if necessary.

'No' is best said firmly, clearly and only as loudly as is appropriate for it to be heard, and then your meaning must be signalled in some way. Remove the object of concern, or turn your back to attend to other things, or stop what you had been doing to see that your command is complied with. For example, you may need to refuse someone an immediate audience with your supervisor, stop someone helping him or herself inappropriately to food, or refuse to pay out money.

> I once accompanied a small boy, Len, to a showground. I had been doing some work with this child who had quite marked emotional and behavioural difficulties and was used to getting his own way with his carers by use of continual pressure and misbehaviour. I had offered to buy Len one chosen item, and following the purchase

I was subject to considerable pressure to buy something more. Every time I said 'no' the pressure increased. We had to stay together as Len was my responsibility for the day. The boy knew this, and it made it easier for him to make the outing miserable for me. However, I continued to make it clear that I would not be swayed.

Eventually Len stopped wheedling and instead had a big temper tantrum, inside a fairly crowded toy marquee, and when he saw I would not give in to the embarrassment of this, he made a threat: 'I won't move from here until you buy me . . .'

This at last gave me an opportunity to reinforce my refusal. 'Fine', I said, 'now I can go and see the things that interest me, and I'll know exactly where to find you when it's time to go.' I turned and rapidly left.

Actually I did not go far, but stayed to observe him from behind the marquee. After a while the anger in Len's face began to fade and he began to walk uncertainly about the marquee. Eventually he came out and began to wander along the fairway between exhibitions. At this point I strode by as if on my way somewhere: 'Ah! There you are', I remarked, 'I'm on my way to the tractor pull. Coming?'

I had no further problems that day.

It is important to remain firm whatever the form of the pressure. If 'no' is said hesitantly it can indicate you may move from your stance if bullied or pestered enough. If 'no' is said too suddenly and loudly it will probably indicate that you are anxious, panicked or frightened, and that more pressure will make you give in. This has important implications for avoiding aggression.

An aggressor may lose control when a response is uncertain as this can reinforce their sense of supremacy in the situation, and they then make greater demands. Similarly when the manner of refusal is open to interpretation it can raise false hopes, and if later a very clear final refusal is made it may provoke a stronger reaction and cause the other person to be sufficiently aggrieved to respond aggressively.

Conversely, other forms of aggression can be disguised pleas for firm boundaries, and by not drawing these clearly, the person's sense of security is weakened, and their search for external controls causes aggression to increase.

Saying 'no' is also important as a mark of a pivotal point. Noting this point if events degenerate is helpful if later there is an inquiry. Your note will illustrate the clarity of your actions and purpose. In some situations it may be appropriate to mark and reinforce the moment of your decision by reminding the other person that you have said 'no', and if ignored, that is their choice of action and thus their responsibility.

'No' needs to be said at an early enough stage when the other person can still respond to the normal rules of behaviour. If a situation is allowed to escalate beyond the point of verbal intervention then the opportunity to avert conflict by words has been missed. Many situations can quickly become a test of resolve, or a sort of blackmail, if the limits have not been made clear. This is particularly so with situations that can develop into a standoff. Uncertain confrontation with groups of excitable, disturbed, or dangerous people can lead to problems associated with crowd mentality, and possibly escalation into lockout or riot type events.

Saying 'no' clearly at an early stage can put a stop to anger developing, but showing uncertainty can result in aggression escalating.

Hurdle-help (9)

Timely help at the moment a barrier to success appears can avoid outbursts of anger.

Frustration is a very common precursor to anger. This typically occurs when a task keeps going wrong, or cannot be started or completed. This phenomenon affects people of all ages and abilities, and in all sorts of situations.

It is unfair to allow a client in need to fall at the hurdles. Halting progress can be too testing of their patience and temper, when their skills, motivation, or self-confidence are weak. Most things happen in sequence, and knowing or best guessing when a helping hand will be needed is the key. A good teacher or instructor will keep a watching distance from the learner, and will know the points at which small assistance will maintain learning progress. Letting others know what and where the hurdles are, and where they will need to make a special effort is good preparation for all sorts of undertakings.

> Jack was a young man with learning difficulties. His programme included life skills for semi-independent living. A target for him was to prepare a simple meal without support. This did not go well when practised. Jack first made a pot of tea but it went cold. His toast kept burning, and then Jack spilt half his beans onto the floor. His frustration became too much. Jack dashed everything to the floor, and he turned to shout and swear at his care worker.

It may help to think how easy it is to bring a person, including yourself, to anger by careless or deliberate action. You may know someone who seems expert at this kind of thing, and been frustrated by them. This person may spring new demands at the last minute, and will let you go on with a wrong procedure or direction. They may drop you in a situation without sufficient preparation, then blame you for non-completion or will remove essential tools, or a vital key. If you know how that feels, then you can feel for others.

Children or adults with learning difficulties who are trying a task may be particularly helped by appropriate intervention. Teachers of children with special educational needs often prepare well for task differentiation, but can overlook the moments that sensitive assistance is required. This intervention has to be before something becomes damaged or discarded in frustration. Failure can easily transmute into conflict that then has to be resolved, and the original problem is overshadowed.

Repeated failure is often part of a chain of experience with the associated negative self-concept and reluctance for endeavour that prevents achievement, such as adults who are afraid to try to overcome their particular difficulties, and children who are alienated from school.

In other situations strangers may need sensitive support. For example, consider people who come into offices to claim a benefit or seek a service. It is important to be sensitive to the person who seems hesitant when faced with a form, as it may be they are not sufficiently literate to cope. Have there been clues, such as did they explain themselves poorly, or somewhat recant the problem when you got out pen and paper? When there is already a problem a new frustration might tip feelings to anger, at themselves, at you, or the totality of their situation. If you suspect difficulties with paperwork step in quickly. Offer to help with a get-out excuse for them by saying how you have a spare moment, or these forms are so poorly designed but you are used to them. Importantly, ask if you can help.

Prevent angry responses by sensitive offers of support.

Permitting (10)

Giving permission for a disruptive activity reduces its attraction.

Conflict often results from attempting to stop something done deliberately to irritate or upset. It also results when something is refused; this is most clearly seen in the two-year-old child who has a temper tantrum when their wants are denied.

Clients who interpret reasonable intervention as a form of personal attack, include people who are ego-damaged, mentally disturbed, or have learning difficulties, and those who are already angry. They will often view the other person as mean or spiteful. Nurses, teachers and carers, all meet instances of escalated aggression following attempts to deny the particular behaviours of those in their care.

It can be helpful in many of these situations to consider whose needs the intervention is for. Often intervention is made because the behaviour challenges authority, or it is irritating, or it will have some minor monetary cost. If no one is in any danger, and no damage is likely, although it may be possible to ignore the disruption, it may be better to *actually give permission* for the behaviour to continue.

Permission giving is particularly relevant if the behaviour is a form of play, or is attention seeking, or a way of establishing trust. This tactic not only considerably reduces the likelihood for conflict, it allows the other person to feel favourably towards you, and this can assist you later with more important demands.

Mary was a girl of thirteen who lived in a children's home. She would often challenge rules, and began to seek permission to go down to a nearby late night corner shop just before her bedtime. This invariably led to arguments, as this time was after normal curfew. Care staff realised she never really needed anything in particular, and the expedition did not offer her any alternative excitement. It represented a challenge to their authority. After several nights of this, a concession was made: Mary could go to the shop at 9.30 provided she asked if others, including staff, needed anything. At first this was quite a nightly ritual, but after a week or two Mary only went to the shop if she was asked.

Importantly, permission removes the potential for the person to feel guilty, from being uncertain about the legitimacy of what they are doing, to what can now be enjoyed without shame. Generalised feelings of anxiety can be lifted and the behaviour of the person will likely remain manageable. If the intention of the client was to be provocative, the attraction of the behaviour is devalued, and it will very likely stop, and the irritation or cost to you ends. If the behaviour was intended to be disruptive, the aggressor is disarmed, although aggressive feelings may show another way.

One caution is when something is requested because it is known it will be denied. This is a trap. It confirms to your client how mean you are, and gives an excuse for aggression. This is used, often subconsciously, by behaviourally disturbed children, and older teenagers when testing their boundaries. With teenagers it can be instructive to give permission by allowing their choice, but with the reminder that there will be consequences that will need to be sorted out or planned for, such as cleaning up afterwards, or arrangements for getting home. Either they will then have second thoughts and not proceed, or they may go ahead and negotiate terms, and this latter option is preferable as it has greater opportunity for self-responsibility.

Workers in public services regularly get confronted by angry people. If a demand is not normally granted or possible at that moment, an outright refusal can lead to argument, and it is better to indicate you will try to support their request, even if this is rather extreme. For example, a demand to see the manager. The first step is to use interpretation and acceptance (Chapter 3) to show you accept the strength of complaint. Agree that they should see the manager, but then explain why this cannot be done now, as the manager is out of the building on his lunch break, at a meeting, or whatever it is. Next, offer alternatives such as waiting, or making an appointment, perhaps seeing another (perhaps more appropriate) manager, or offer your own help. The opportunity for decision-making will appear to the client as retaining control, and even if they are still unco-operative, very likely they are now less aggressive in manner, and more open to negotiation.

Reduce the potential for conflict, and devalue disruptive behaviour by concession.

This section has presented ten techniques for use in person-to-person situations, how to respond to aggressive disruption, and to reduce its impact. The techniques are valuable skills for anyone concerned with managing anger and aggressive behaviour in others. The techniques are appropriate for use within a range of situations, and with a variety of client types, but the use of any one will require some professional discrimination regarding its relevance and how it is applied in the particular circumstances.

All the techniques have therapeutic potential. They are most effective when their use is so practised that they become part of your professional persona and are applied fluidly.

Chapter 3

Wordy Techniques

The following two techniques involve spoken and written intervention that is less immediate, but is thought through by client and worker. The techniques will help mollify sources of worry, reduce confusions and uncertainties, and help put the practitioner and the client in better control of the issues concerned.

Acceptance and interpretation (11)

Verbalising aggressive feelings and having them heard will make it less likely they are acted out. Expressing anger externalises the emotion. Appropriate responses reduce inner tension and the compulsion to act.

This technique is effective with angry or destructive emotions as it helps their safe discharge and reduces the potential for feelings to worsen. It is one of the most useful techniques in this book, and anyone who has had training to work at a complaints desk will recognise its elements. It uses a counselling technique to allay anxiety, and by sorting out confusions it helps redress poor processing of information.

Anger management training usually emphasises that it is a mistake to allow people to overly ventilate their feelings, but is often less clear about what this means. It is seldom productive to allow an angry client to come to a pitch of emotion, but neither are they helped if their anger is met by rebuff, deflection, or denial. This can provoke greater rage and entrench their viewpoint. Responses that duck the client's issues only cause them to carry further resentment that they were not accorded sensitive treatment or a proper hearing. And anger, regularly repressed, is linked with the development of depression.

Feelings must find expression. This technique is about accepting and assisting with the feelings of the moment. Acceptance and interpretation is not ventilation, it is much more positive (see also Introduction: **CARMA**, and Chapter 8: Silence and Paraphrasing). There are three distinct stages:

Acceptance: immediate empathy

People who are angry or in a distressed state can be helped if you openly show you recognise their distress. Say something like: 'I can see you are upset'. Even if you may feel you are stating the obvious, putting their emotion into words signals that you are empathetic to an obvious presentation or picked up on their emotional cues. Their upset is eased by the security and containment suggested by your reassurance and acceptance of their condition.

The acceptance of the client is shown by your receptivity to them however they present themselves. This may mean allowing them to 'jump a queue', or, for example, not rebuffing them by saying they must calm down before you will help. Many clients in addition to the anger will also carry anxiety that they will not be given sufficient consideration. Upfront acceptance strongly signals your honesty and robustness, which helps the client place their trust in you for the next stage: interpretation.

Interpretation: sorting out the issues

Ask what you can do to help. Use accepting and interpretative comment to paraphrase the situation or the feelings. This is already soothing and empathy giving. The provision of your external source of calm to them provides a screen of security within which their complaint or feelings can be explored and words found to properly describe their problem. The client is helped to shape a miasma of anger into something specific that can be dealt with. During this time their body and mind can relax and they will return to a more normal emotional state. Expect their breathing to become more even, and their voice become more moderate in tone as these physiological conditions begin to mirror yours.

Talking and using other word constructs gives the client an opportunity to gain the emotional or knowledge vocabulary related to their problem. Firstly this aids their self-expression. Secondly, finding ways of properly ascribing reasons for the anger, and labelling the sources, reduces the chaos. Putting names to things will help a client feel more in control, and is an essential precursor to effective dealing with them, and having some power over them. This leads to the last stage.

Action

When you and your client have identified and agreed a description of the problem, sensible action can be formulated. When you are able to say for your client what the problem is, the issue has become externalised from them. It now has a form of its own when it has been accepted and given new expression. Written down, the issue becomes formalised and even strong anxiety can give way to relief or better anticipation. The resolution is usually a course of action that can actually be written down rather like a flow chart or set of instructions (see next technique: Mapping).

Sheila worked behind the counter at the Social Security office. A woman came in and was visibly distressed at the length of the queues. When she got to the counter her words were garbled and she could not say what she wanted. In her frustration she stood, sending her chair flying back, and waved some papers in Sheila's face.

Sheila gently took her arm and eased it down: *'You are very upset. Something is making you angry. Is it something this is about?'* Sheila took the papers, the woman nodded, her teeth clenched.

'Then let me read them. May I? It will help me see why you are upset – what the problem is. Why don't you sit for a moment? It's OK. Give me a minute or two and then we can work out how I can help.'

Sheila was able to reassure her client, and deal with her problems, although not much could be done immediately, and not what the woman wanted, but she was able to trust Sheila, and the situation progressed more calmly because of Sheila's accepting and unruffled manner.

Sheila also wrote out the problems and their sequence. This gave time for the woman to become composed, and time for the woman's actual worry to be separated from the tension stemming from her wait. The process cleared up some procedural matters, and the woman had to accept that she had ignored some of these, and had made the situation worse than it might have otherwise been. The process also allowed the main problem to be identified, and when the woman saw this more clearly she began to use the same words and expressions Sheila had used.

This technique is an invaluable way of responding to other people when the origin of their anger is uncertain. It is also a moral way to respond as it values the other person and their reality and feelings. Their personal autonomy is encouraged by you accepting the cause of their anger, and by seeking a solution with, rather than for, them. Assistance moves from accepting their anger to attaching proper labels to events and feelings, sorting out relevant issues, and organising these into a coherent structure. This kind of assistance empowers the other person and calms their emotion.

Perversely some processes can unfortunately prevent the proper resolution to problems – it goes so far, but fails to deliver. It seems sometimes that is the intention. Some formal complaints procedures are so elaborated that their process negates what they are intended to provide. The lengthy and formal way some complaints are processed is presumably intended to ensure the core issue is properly arrived at, and resolved; but it can be used to bury it because processes that gain complexity or take too long will risk losing relevance to the client, or test their resolve. The procedure may be so laborious that it is impossible to sustain the intensity of emotion that drove the complaint in the first place. People give up, or their lives move on.

Giving up is especially the response of children because their lives are driven quickly by new events, experiences, and emotions. The 1989 Children Act had good intent in regard to the development of complaints procedures for children in public care. But many complaints are often not realised to completion, or the issue is resolved in some other way, sometimes only because in the meantime the child has been accommodated elsewhere, or their self-concern shifts to something new (good or bad).

Red tape and lengthy processes can filter off many clients not fully determined, or not supported by advocacy or other assistance in pursuit of their complaint. The process is misused when delayed or a 'buy-off' compromise eventually offered, rather than making a response in a more honest or prompt form.

Local Authorities vary in the quality of their procedures and resources, and on how quickly they free up or otherwise allocate a complaints officer from among their social work team; and whether or not they have active child rights officers who are fully client centred. Anyone who is party to delay or diversion when responding to clients who are angry or distressed may be colluding (see Chapter 7: Collusion).

Having anger accepted and acknowledged is therapeutic. Resolution can result when help is given to describe the source of anger and decide upon proper action.

Mapping (12)

Anticipating problems, preparation, and sorting issues provides guidance to clients by effective routes through procedures and choices.

Most people have experienced the frustration of being lost or delayed when trying to arrive on time at an important destination. Is there a driver who has not felt angry at traffic, fog, poor directions, or the lack of a map? The likely sources of road rage are too commonly experienced, but fortunately few of us express it directly. Less commonplace is that someone else has ensured you have sufficient extra time for an uncertain journey, or gone out of their way to ensure you have good directions. Mapping does this for 'life journeys'; it is a more structured form of Hurdle-help (Chapter 2).

Mapping can prevent anger resulting from an inability to achieve an objective, or when anger is the way anxiety or frustration is vented. A watch can be made for clients who are vulnerable, or are approaching a point where a problem might arise. Mapping is a form of anger management that depends on reducing the probability of an outburst by preparing clients for foreseeable difficulties and by providing them with forms of guidance.

This technique should be a regular way of working with clients at risk of temper loss, or when a situation is likely to be a severe test of client self-control. Mapping for individual clients depends on knowing what each finds difficult, and making appropriate preparation. Usually this includes talking through and anticipation, it may involve role-play and practice.

For example, a client who has over-familiarity and trust of strangers is equipped with a list of 'do's and don'ts', and practices appropriate conversation, and safe responses.

Mapping for situations depends on knowing what the common difficulty is and ensuring that all clients are prepared. A simple example from residential care is adequate preparation prior to an inspection visit, and ensuring clients know about it and do not become anxious or defensive about an enquiry as to how they live and are treated. An example from juvenile justice social work is the preparation of young persons if they are to cope well with the experience of court, particularly if they are to give evidence. Much social and life skills teaching is about structured anticipation of hurdles to come, and providing dry runs and role plays, from simple things like using the phone in an emergency to preparing for a job interview or a difficult meeting. A caring worker will provide analogies to help explain difficult proceedings, and will talk through what has to be done.

The technique is to ensure the client fully understands what is required; and not to accept their word but get the narrative repeated. 'Verbalising the action' helps understanding to be internalised and ensures comprehension. Additional help can be provided by written or diagrammatic material. Typically this involves the sequences or stages of a system or how a procedure works, and assistance is provided by a prompt card or systems map. Such material may be for the bespoke personal use of individual clients or with generic matters be worked up as a display poster or information card. The mapping must include means to progress time or stages by use of numbers or dates in a sequence – even simple pictures if the client has poor literacy. The action at the end of **CARMA** may be a form of mapping.

The map format should show the client, or support their understanding of, where they are –at what point in any procedure or process. It must highlight the decision points. The use of flow charts, or lists with tick or date boxes are a useful way to organise, and these provide a way for clients to keep track for themselves of things they have to do, and the supervisor is given an instant update. Include feedback loops in the flow of instructions so that the client can be referred back to supervisory support should they need this.

Sometimes the 'map' has to be kept for the client because of learning, or physiological, or other difficulties they may have. In such instances it offers a record of the points of reference between the two persons involved and supports shared ownership of the client-supervisor process. It is essential the client is re-involved should any deviation have to be made, or if there is any delay. A map may not be completely foolproof.

Den was a young man with learning difficulties. He wanted to lead a small group of students with similar problems to a venue in Liverpool, primarily because the rail journey was one he often travelled and felt confident about, but it soon became clear he was worried about the short walk upon arrival. He could not manage an actual map, and was anxious about asking strangers for directions. A lot of preparation was done before the day, and the route memorised.

In the event he and his group arrived late. Den was in an agitated state and he immediately began to assault his care worker. Den felt his instructions had failed him. Later it became clear Den had memorised perfectly, but he had exited from the station differently from where his care worker assumed, and consequently then set off in the wrong direction. Fortunately Den kept the self-confidence the preparation had given him, and he had continued to lead his group although lost. His winding perambulations eventually gave him sight of the monument he recognised as the venue and he was able to walk directly to it.

The care worker was able later to praise Den for coping, but it was some time before he regained Den's trust, and before Den's self-confidence returned. They both learnt.

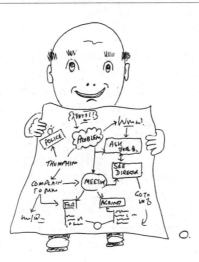

Mapping is preparing clients with routes through difficulties and providing a plan to follow.

Chapter 4

Managing Techniques

These techniques are more elaborate. People are considered in conjunction with their environments for ways aggressive behaviour and its impact on others may be minimised. The first three techniques have superficial similarity but are discrete.

Restructuring (13)

Restructuring deals with deteriorating relationships by a change of environment – of people, place, or activity.

Imagine a party at which a particular couple attend, and one partner, through drink or boredom, is just beginning to be rather maudlin. This may get offensive if it continues, but the second person takes control with a firm decision, and taking their partner they make their grace and leave. This scenario presents, literally, the sensible decision to leave a party while it is still being enjoyed. It is the simplest of techniques with a potential for 100 per cent effectiveness in avoiding conflict and being struck off the guest list.

Restructuring is making change to environmental conditions such as the parameters, membership, or location. It usually includes considerations about things like space, rotas, venues, numbers of people, length of time, or frequency of repetition.

Responsibility for the people worked with often includes deciding about attending events. Some clients will get vicarious enjoyment from the stress of others or will bully or dominate situations. These must be quickly restructured and not provided again without sufficient preparatory work. Upset because an activity is allowed to continue for too long, can often be foreseen by proper consideration of past experience, professional judgement, and ongoing observation. It may be appropriate to make formal risk assessment.

On occasions when something has deteriorated into conflict, it is not the fun that was had that is remembered, but the tears, the guilt, and the problems of making redress. Bad experiences lead to negative self-constructs, and the result can include loss of confidence for both staff and clients, whilst the client's self-esteem may be the most damaged, or anxieties increased, the particular activities will lose attraction for both sets of people.

The consequences of insensitivity or poor forethought can be extreme.

Jess was a young man who had led a very deprived life. He was inappropriately taken as part of a small group outing to a prestigious presentation of a Shakespearean play. Culturally, the play was fairly meaningless to him. Many people were in evening dress. Jess made some protestation about boredom after the play had begun but I ignored him. Despite the fact that it became quite clearly a long and demanding experience for him, no respite was offered, and I was hesitant to leave the rest of my group. Jess kept up his very best behaviour and managed not to disturb his companions nor the rest of the audience. The price of this to him was only revealed when the play ended and his party were in the street outside the theatre. Jess, who had contained himself so well, experienced some kind of breakdown. He let out frenzied screams and dropped to the pavement jerking his limbs. Initially, Jess violently attacked anyone who came near him.

Marvellously, Jess never lost his trust in me. Now, with experience, I would have left the group and taken Jess out for a long coffee or two. But as a young man at the outset of my career, this event taught me to never take the wisdom of my superiors for granted; on this occasion, about the suitability of the event, the group composition, and appropriate staffing levels.

There are two main ways to restructure; the focus is either the activity or the social mix.

Restructuring the activity

This means taking responsibility and making decisions. The emphasis on the dynamics of a situation may mean putting a stop to it, or going elsewhere, ideally as action rather than reaction, and before any undesirable event occurs. Use a reasoned excuse, or diversionary tactics, but not to suggest that you think a conflict is about to happen. This may provoke denial, draw you into actual conflict, or reinforce negative perceptions.

If comment has to be made it is better to keep this positive rather than draw attention to the limitations of individuals. For example, when interactions are becoming charged to say 'I think we need a change' or 'this seems to be boring you now, let's go and do something else . . .' is much less negative than to comment directly or provocatively upon the deteriorating relationships; i.e. 'we'd better go before you get into a fight'. Focusing upon the activity recognises that an activity has become too challenging, or not sufficiently engaging. The relevance of the activity provides a different view than highlighting client limitations. Activity evaluation usually requires a decision, that is, responsibility for the activity, or an intervention, an involvement in client choice. Even if problems do occur, it will help the client to save face if the activity is blamed (because it is too long, difficult or inappropriate).

Teachers use restructuring all the time to maintain the vitality of pupil interest. One illustration is group reading. The teacher gauges the level of concentration and motivation in their pupils, and will stop reading before the point when they have become too restless. Pupils with the greatest behavioural difficulty, or whose interest is least, are most likely to come into early conflict with their teacher or a classmate if the class is generally becoming unsettled or disengaged. If a class has been still and quiet for a while, a more active task is usually introduced, and subsequently, reading or some other quiet work will be easier to resume; and the vulnerable pupils protected from their own limitations.

Restructuring the group membership

Consideration of the personality mix may suggest removing an individual or a set of members. This can be a short-term measure or a more permanent response. Restructuring to help stop relationships from deteriorating can be a subtle intervention such as offering something more desirable, or sending someone on an errand, or be more wide reaching by interceptive division or exclusion. Examples of intervention include changes of pairings, class-group, outing companions, table companions, or even a change of institution.

Restructuring is the key way to ensure conflict between two antagonistic persons is avoided, as it reduces or ends their proximity to each other. It can also help preclude the emergence of a dominant or a subservient member within groups. Sometimes offering a change or some reason to move on is all that is required.

A crisis intervention care home for a small group of teenagers is well equipped. One evening the play on the pool table was getting too competitive; and the attitude of one of the players, Andy, was becoming very aggressive and confrontational. This was mostly directed at David who had a history of violent behaviour, and was trying to leave this behind him, but did not want to lose face. A care worker who had been keeping an eye on developments 'reminded' David there was a good film on TV that they had talked about watching together. There was a quick agreement from David because the suggestion represented an acceptable escape route from a deteriorating situation.

Be aware of the effect of different physical and social environments, and restructure these as necessary.

Bouncing (14)

Keeping dynamics fluid so that conflicts do not have time to emerge.

A way of dealing with a client who is constantly in conflict is to keep relationships, or the situation, so novel that difficulties or anti-social behaviours do not have the opportunity to surface. Bouncing means continually moving this person from one environment to another – a form of continuous restructuring. The opportunity for conflicts to emerge is much reduced when there is continual change to surroundings or companions.

Bouncing can be invaluable when there is a shortage of staff, or an organisation is stretched to the limits of its response, and when there are not the resources or the time to respond in a more proper and therapeutic manner. Bouncing will help reduce risk when there is a significant danger of physical harm, either of the subject self-harming, or assault upon others. Bouncing one client may benefit the overall effectiveness of work with a larger group and avoid compromising the work with others. It can save routines from constant interruption from a run of incidents, and can avoid behaviour contagion when peers become 'contaminated' and they also begin to be difficult to manage.

Bouncing can be particularly useful managing people with very low self-esteem or low expectations of life. They may be looking for their negative self-constructs to be confirmed, and aggressive behaviour is a way of ensuring this. They will seek conflict by picking fights, spoiling their work, or making unpleasant or provocative comment. Bouncing can reduce the frequency of difficult incidents, with useful outcomes. The intervention will help keep client behaviour fairly static while a response from other agencies is organised, such as counselling, placement review, or a new plan. A reduction of the actual number of incidents may make other work with the client more possible as there are not lots of problematic outcomes to deal with first. And change to the client 'case history' makes it more possible to present the client more positively to others and the client self by means of new evaluation.

Managing the environment and bouncing to reduce conflict incident is unfortunately sometimes a cheap management technique or a disguised punishment, as may be the case when clients are moved from one accommodation to another. The concern always is to ensure that the integrity of an individual's programme is maintained. The technique is misused when this is an easy way of managing people with problems, or because staffs do not have the inclination or skills to address the real issues (see Chapter 7, Collusion).

It is important to protect the rapport of the individual with the group. Bouncing may affect the subject's status, and the intervention may cause them to be seen as a *scapegoat* or *as hero* with further difficulties that ensue from this. Preparation may be appropriate before the reintroduction of the subject to the original group.

The technique is not new. A colleague who made use of this technique to occasionally manage difficult dynamics would refer to it as the Makarenko principle (Makarenko, 1951).

Makarenko worked in pre-Stalinist Russia. Fired with a belief he could help build a new social order, his job was to take on some of the most extremely damaged young people who were being rounded up off the streets during the early 1920s. These were delinquents and vagabonds, some of whom had been saved from the firing squad, and he was given a revolver to use if needing to protect himself and others. Makarenko's farm camp was very successful, and represented an early attempt at a self-regulating therapeutic community. To reduce conflict and personality clashes between the most volatile of the young men, Makarenko constantly moved particular individuals from group to group, or from task to task, often with a pretext that built up self-esteem.

If a client is belligerent, keeping them 'on the move' can prevent conflicts from developing, and reduce the frequency of incident.

Regrouping (15)

Regrouping is linked to restructuring and bouncing, but with a very different emphasis. It is used to reduce predictable conflict conditions by emphasis for the 'positive merits' that clients can obtain from a new situation, and with longer-term prospects in mind. Regrouping is a deliberate attempt to optimise interpersonal conditions; but not by managing conflict by simple division or exclusion.

Regrouping requires understanding the group dynamics and knowledge of the people involved, in order to structure groupings for beneficial relationships, such as a client's association with a desirable role model. It is usually a more considered intervention than the previous two techniques, and is done mainly in response to good knowledge about the needs and difficulties of the clients concerned, and for other merits the proposal may include.

Regrouping determines the membership of groups based on positive constructs. Importantly, how are decisions arrived at and how are they presented? Here is a simple situation:

A youth group was travelling in a minibus to a theme park. They had some conflict on the journey, a fight broke out, and the bus had to stop. The party fell into two opposing camps. The accompanying youth leader decided it would be best if the group were spilt up between himself and his co-workers upon arrival at their destination. Keeping apart those who had taken opposing stances could have obtained a workable division, this would be restructuring. Restructuring to retain the two 'camps' in this way would reinforce their division, and by maintaining the split, reinforce the prejudice that led to the conflict. The conflict would likely be renewed when the whole group reconvened.

Instead the leader decided to take the opportunity to regroup. This was done in a matter-of-fact way, and based on good relationships and interest criteria. Members from each 'camp' were formed into three subgroups, each representing an interest subset, and kept some individuals attached to their preferred youth worker (and this reasoning was given, without much mention of the journey difficulties). Key antagonists were kept apart, but otherwise 'camp' members were integrated. Sharing the destination event and some quiet words during the day from the youth leaders attached to the two main protagonists allowed the rest of the day and the return journey to pass much more sociably.

Decisions taken with regard to the well-being, or in the best interest generally of members are most likely to be supported by a group. Responding by a punitive restructuring, by identifying one or more group members as the main antagonists and insisting on close supervision, is demeaning. It reinforces undesirable self-perceptions and implies others are better in comparison. It also does not invite self-control.

Regrouping is counterproductive if a client is placed where their wishes or needs are ignored. If clients are projected as scapegoats or bullies this will entrench their role, and the prophecy that is implied will increase the likelihood of further conflict.

Regrouping puts people together for the positive benefits of their shared company.

Avoiding a void (16)

Anxiety or immediate anger can increase in situations where response is hesitant.

If an aggressor confronts you and you step back in confusion or embarrassment, the aggressor will step forward, as their tactics are working. Alternatively if you rally defensively, a counter-threat at this stage may escalate the situation. How best to deal with situations is also very dependent on your confidence and how assertive you are in difficult situations. This is very much an important area for training, role-play, and discussion rather than being gleaned from a book, but it is easy enough to understand that clients who are distressed by anxiety, or angry and verging on aggression do not respond well to uncertainty. Although they may care what the consequences are if they lose self-control, if their grip is fragile, uncertainty will be a 'flash point' for them. Distressed people often need external forms of control. Without it anxiety increases, and will show as aggression in the search for help and containment. With angry clients hesitancy can be seen as a weakness to be taken advantage of, and their aggression will also increase.

The client may have come to you with some problem, or you have walked in on an incident. Hesitancy will risk many situations worsening. This may be shown at a subliminal level by body language or more consciously by uncertain comment or other sign. You are immediately part of the dynamics, and, if only for a brief moment or two, you have the initiative. Take it and fill the void.

The technique is the important recognition that this is the moment for response and the effectiveness and relevance of what follows will be linked to how quickly you react. The technique does not rely on particular sets of responses, but upon your initiation of a response, sometimes almost any response will do! Even when very uncertain, remember it is usually better to do or say something; a change of tack can come later as ideas develop or a better thought occurs.

An appropriate response may well be one of the techniques already presented, particularly Acceptance and Interpretation (Chapter 3). Some techniques may be combined. It can be helpful to gain a thinking space, or prepare the ground for more than one route, or provide some feedback to indicate the way to continue. One way is to combine Acceptance and Interpretation with Appeal (Chapter 2). 'Paraphrase' and 'verbalise' the aggressor's problem calmly and with assurance, and at the same time give a controlling or 'appeal' message, such as: 'Hey, I can see you're really cross. You're cross with . . . but hold up, I can't concentrate when you shout like that. I want to help'.

Another combination is 'humour' with 'saying no'. This can be a very effective way of asserting firm external control in a very non-threatening way. This is often done naturally when it reflects the personality and confidence of the user.

One of the most difficult work settings is a major hospital Accident and Emergency reception, particularly on a busy Saturday night. The routines are not always acceptable to those who are intoxicated, or highly anxious or simply selfish, hence the instant drama of TV programmes such as 'Casualty'. The usual practice of moving people

> along from reception to a waiting area and then to a cubicle helps signal to people that they are in process. The safest teams are those that mutually support each other in their work and have a high degree of social contact with each other, and with the public, as they pass along the system so that voids are minimised.

Always respond to people immediately, and assert your control upon their anger.

Promises and rewards (17)

Consistency is the key to effective use of reward in anger management.

Promises and rewards are extrinsic ways of motivating desired behaviour. They are particularly useful to reinforce strategies that may have been given to clients to help them cope with their feelings of anger as part of their anger management (i.e. counting to ten, or breathing exercises).

Rewards tend to be associated with short term, or specific objectives. Examples are: a child has to earn so many ticks for not shouting at peers during a lesson in order to choose a treat at break time; a social worker promises a young person a Macdonald's lunch if they manage a difficult review meeting in the way they have prepared.

Rewards are useful for clients whose understanding of the world is chaotic, or whose ego is so poorly developed they are unable to make adequate links between their behaviour and its consequences so that good things happen by chance, or they have to be snatched at as they pass by. Use of rewards is meant to teach cause and effect, and this must be 'consistent', and for behaviour that the subject can comprehend and control. (See also Chapter 4, Punishment.)

It is essential that promises be only made when it is known they can be kept, so it does not matter whether these are unconditional or a reward. Breaking promises destroys trust. It reaffirms to the client that their chaotic or pessimistic viewpoint is correct, about you, about others generally, the world, and their self-worth. This will increase the way they feel they are mistreated, and they will respond to their world in a rejecting and aggressive manner.

Ultimately, what you are trying to teach is that desirable, more sociable behaviour will bring its own intrinsic rewards. The levels of emotional and intellectual development are key factors to be assessed before any reward system is introduced. This requires that the behaviour and any associated system of rewards are relevant to the person concerned.

For a child of two this may mean learning about adult imposed rules and boundaries, perhaps about not hitting peers, or not showing temper by throwing things. Rewards will be simple and within very short time spans. At twelve years, the concern may still be about rules and boundaries, but has moved on to more sophisticated levels, and it is appropriate for behaviour now to have stronger internal loci. Rewards may now be self-referred, and be at longer intervals. For an adult the reward may be something they have promised to themselves, for example, someone receiving relationship counselling may plan a celebratory meal if they have managed the week without violence to their partner.

A reward is relevant only when the behaviour is objective and possible to be self-controlled.

Joe is a young adult who has challenging behaviour and lives in an specialised care home. Staff discussed his programme with a consultant. They wanted to offer Joe a cinema trip on Thursdays provided that he'd 'had a good day'. What this meant could not be described very usefully, and if implemented was more likely to reinforce Joe's negative constructs, about staff and himself, should the poorly specified criteria not be met. The consultant helped point up appropriate expectations. Joe was told that the workshop supervisor had to report that he had completed the morning without arguing with him, and at tea time Joe had to report to a careworker that he had managed the afternoon without hitting Freddie, his usual companion. This was possible for Joe, and measurable enough. Anything else would be ignored in consideration for the cinema outing.

There are other ways to respond to people who behave like Joe. Someone who has a well-established relationship, a 'significant other', with the client, could observe and identify a good day for them. This is then drawn to their attention, and the client helped to see why the day has gone well. Talking provides the words and the ideas about desired behaviour. Improved behaviour is sought, and by helping to internalise the relevant values and choices the client is supported towards more acceptable autonomous actions. The process may involve repetition, or focus on only a limited range of behaviour, and time to explore and explain. To help the client self-manage, a chart may be started to track the frequency or the subject of his outbursts, and a reward system is set up in conjunction with this.

Praise and recognition are rewarding, and powerful ways to reinforce desired behaviours. The achievement must be marked in an appropriate way, whether this is a quiet 'well done' or is more celebratory. Comparative comments are best avoided. To commend a client that they are the 'quickest worker', or the 'most trusted', implies others are less worthy, and may cause others to be jealous or spiteful. Comment that is tied to absolutes provides little encouragement for the behaviour to develop more globally in the client, and it can create a loss of esteem if the client falls short of the absolute, and invites others to challenge rather than copy it. Far better to simply make an observation, for example, 'You didn't get cross with X did you? Well done. I'm very pleased with you'. Or, 'It's a great help when there is someone to be trusted to go to the post office for me . . .'

Empathy on failure and rejoicing over success is an essential positive association with the client about their experiences in gaining personal and social ground, and of belonging to humanity. Relationships, intrinsically, are prime movers. If someone has no interest in sharing the client's ups and downs then better they buy a whistle and go and train dogs.

Rewards used in a consistent and consequential manner are effective in changing behaviour.

The next two techniques are the most controversial and can raise many operational issues. Despite this they are valid for consideration and this book would be incomplete without their inclusion, although with physical restraint only issues are presented.

Punishment, consequences and threats (18)

The power to punish others is a great but questionable responsibility.

Punishment

The use of punishment is usually for one of three reasons:

1. **Retribution:** this may result from the pressure of society, say a penal code, or may reflect the inadequacies of a system or the people with authority, in that either they are vengeful in character, or how they respond is based on ideas about pay-back.

2. **Substitution:** punishment is often the easiest response to implement. As an imposed consequence it has an adverse or negating effect on what the other person intended as a result of their behaviour. Substitution alters the reward end of a cycle of behaviour.

3. **A warning to others:** a first condition for punishment to have any constructive effect is that the recipient and those it is intended to warn are not to be confused by it. It must be just and warranted, and understood and accepted as deserved as a consequence of active, anti-social choice. The punishment must clearly relate to behaviour in an area possible for the transgressor to control; and for those it warns to understand about. For example, it would be both cruel and inappropriate to punish an eneuretic child who has a medical condition, or to delay punishment beyond the point where the recipient can connect it to their behaviour.

For many people punishment may be testing in the very area in which they are often most disturbed, or have outstanding developmental or nurturing needs. Punishment that confuses people damages their ego-function. Children who have been emotionally or psychologically abused, and people with learning difficulties, illustrate the groups for whom punishment is seldom appropriate. Older dysfunctional children receiving punishment might view it as unprovoked aggression to which a retaliatory response must be made, or it feeds their self-perception of victimisation. Children who have been cared for chaotically, and who lack positive internalised values, can reason that punishment is what adults inflict in order to make them biddable to their will.

Punishment can have unintended outcomes if the client pathology is uncertain. It can reinforce psychotic thought, and be interpreted as more proof of being surrounded by hostile people. It may be internalised non-specifically as another confirmation of personal ineffectiveness, or a lack of worth and undesirability, and thus help secure the foundations for a wide range of unfortunate pathologies.

Punishment has, de facto, to occur after the event, and is externally imposed. It does little to help others manage their anger or aggression. Indeed, it may precipitate a battle of wills, create barriers around clients, or make the aggressor turn to more covert expressions.

Jenny was a young and inexperienced mother with two young children. Ben was the younger, and as a sickly child actually needed a lot of attention. Cathy, the elder child, was still very emotionally dependent, and increasingly found herself in competition with Ben for her mother's attention. Little was done by Jenny to give Cathy any special time, or to include her in caring for Ben. Jenny found that Cathy became a nuisance to her when caring for Ben, and when her pestering began to be accompanied by a high pitched whine, Jenny began the habit of slapping Cathy about the legs and driving her away. Ben began to receive unexplained injuries.

Eventually the sibling jealousy and rage that Cathy felt, and the blame she ascribed to Ben for her neglect, grew to the point that Ben was badly hurt by her, and she in turn severely punished. At this point, fortunately, help was extended to Jenny.

The inappropriateness of Jenny's responses will be evident to people with any experience of raising children, or understanding of child development. Although unfortunately there are many mothers who act like Jenny, responses like Jenny's are occasionally made by persons who are paid to know better.

Consequences

Punishment is reactive. When it is possible to be pro-active, consequences are normally fully appropriate. Consequences get the other person considering their actions. Presenting consequences to an aggressor implies they can make a choice and helps to bring their focus of thought onto themselves, rather than on another's action which is the case when punishment is given. Even although consequences are usually imposed, they can be presented in a clear manner as alternatives. To use consequences implies some dialogue about conditions and criteria. Consequences are usually presented when both parties still enjoy a more dispassionate frame of mind than when punishment is about to be given.

In the case of Jenny, among other measures, she was shown how to reduce Cathy's whining habit by lining up Smarties for Cathy when she had to attend to Ben during the day. The number of sweets was increased or reduced depending on how Cathy had helped her Mum to be free of 'hurting ears' by whining or not whining. In this respect the consequence had two paths, both within Cathy's options for choice. Reduction of sweets was a form of punishment, but they could otherwise as easily be earned, and Cathy's desirable behaviour rewarded. The number of sweets represented negative and positive reinforcements towards her change of behaviour and Jenny was also advised to sit with Cathy and feed the sweets to her.

Sandra worked for the Education Tuition Services of a local authority. Her pupils were mostly teenage boys who had been excluded from school. Some of these had histories of violence, and drink or substance abuse. She used rooms in community centres to teach in that were near to her pupils.

On one occasion a pupil had come in following a drinking bout and had been causing difficulties. Circumstances were such that later she found herself alone with this youth who came into the office area and demanded to use the phone. There were house rules about the use of the phone. A confrontation ensued in which he grabbed Sandra's wrists and threatened to smash them on the desk edge and break her arms. Sandra could not protect herself against his superior strength, but she responded by acknowledging the boy could do this, but this would be the only way he would get to use the phone. Sandra calmly outlined how severe the consequences would be for them both, and suggested other courses of action. After a moment of hesitation the boy flung loose Sandra's arms and stormed out of the building.

Timing is important. Delay causes punishment or consequence to lose relevance. This is particularly the case with young children, when child behaviour and the corresponding adult action have to be closely associated for learning to occur. It is essential that consequences are controllable by the subject by their choice of behaviour, and they follow sufficiently closely, whether for desired or undesired behaviour.

Consequences have to be appropriate and relevant: reduce aggression by offering a choice of consequences before it occurs.

Threats

Threats are a description of what a bad consequence or punishment might be. If a consequence is offered only as a 'might be', or is inconsistently applied, then all that is being taught is the inconsistency of the adult or authority concerned. A threat can sound like a challenge to test resolve. This differs from a clear statement about a consequence. Consider the difference between:

If the lounge is not tidied up, or if I have to do it, I might not take you to the cinema.

and:

The lounge must be tidied up first if we are to go to the cinema. I have no intention of having to dash in the traffic if I'm delayed because I have to do this chore. 7.15 is the deadline.

Conclusion

Punishment figures highly in many establishments despite what they may profess. However, this is an area where conventions of understanding are shifting, and people who at one time did not have their civil rights considered, or had parity disregarded, are increasingly drawn into equality of the law. Children, and people with learning, or mental health difficulties are current examples that illustrate this, and the growth in advocacy services, and consideration of legislation as therapeutically jurisprudent for these clients is evidence of change.

How children would come to be viewed was well expressed by Lord Mackay:

A major philosophical change in recent years has been the way in which both society and the law have looked at the child. The child is now seen more as a person and less as . . . an object of concern. The more a child is seen as a person the more it makes sense to talk of rights.

Rights are now well enshrined in a range of legislation, and all public planning for individual children must provide opportunity for their wishes and opinions to be considered *once they have age or ability that makes it possible for them to express a view*. One common punishment for children is the use of detention in schools. This has been rather a grey area legally, and schools have relied on co-operation with parents. It is very possible that detention will cease to be used, despite prescription for it in the 1997 Education Act; it represents an incursion into civil liberties. Detaining a group or a class for the misdemeanour of one or two pupils is already very ill-advised.

Physical punishment is currently a big issue of political correctness (see Chapter 7, Scapegoating). Physical punishment of children is now against the law (although case precedent is still unclear on parental physical punishment) and the UK now compares better with how European countries view punishing children. A good résumé of the legalities of physical punishment was given in *Community Care* (27.11.97: 10-1).

It is important to work out where you stand, and what effect any punishment interventions you make may have on reducing or even increasing conflict:

• Punishment has a limited role in controlling aggression in others.

• Consequences can be a useful part of treatment.

• Threats can be questioned and are questionable.

Physical restraint (19)

Physical restraint must be the last technique to use.

The ultimate form of control is restraint, and it is the last technique here. Although it is not possible here to advise on physical restraint, some issues may be considered.

Work situations are very variable and authorities such as Health, Social Services and Education Departments issue guidelines appropriate for their institutions. It is an area where the government is showing increased interest, but the various advisory documents it issues give only general guidance and are very poor in showing how restraint is to be achieved. Workers should be wary of employment situations where restraining others is likely to occur but no training or guidance is given.

Restraint is universally advised only when all else has failed, indeed, police training emphasises the use of communications skills to assert control in a situation before resorting to physical contact. It is against health and safety laws for people to be expected to use force or even the more passive forms of restraint if they are not trained to do so. If any worker is in a situation where they may have to physically restrain other people there must be written guidelines and training given. These should inform **when, how, and what** restraint is used.

Training instructs on the techniques of restraint, and how to avoid injury to oneself and others. This is the paramount concern for workers who may have to restrain clients or service users – particularly if these are children, or otherwise vulnerable adults. Restraint is best actually demonstrated, and regularly practised, under proper supervisory instruction, and is routine for personnel such as the police and prison staff.

Sometimes an event gives rise to a call for staff to have training for restraint. However, the issue is not straightforward. Obviously, safe holds, moves, and breakaways can be taught and practiced, but the calm conditions of the training room are very different from the environment and emotion of a workplace incident. This will typically be after some difficult and tense making antecedents, and the restraint will likely take place in an awkward or confined space or surrounded by problematic fittings and furniture, and possibly a hostile audience. Safe restraint is learnt by familiarity and practice. This is only obtained in workplaces where the use of restraint is sufficiently familiar to obtain experience. In all other situations half-remembered stale training may be more hindrance than help. Hesitancy and talk will be safer than action unless the action is very assured. There is also some evidence to suggest that when staffs have had restraint training the use of restraint increases – presumably at the cost of other responses and the skills that go along with less physical interventions.

It is important to be aware of the issues that restraint may provoke. These are usually related to the power differentials between the parties involved, and include race, gender, and age, and relative strengths, say, of adults versus children. Common sense and common law supports the view that it is not valid to use force to save a few pounds of damage, or as a response to provocation that is not causing actual physical harm. Injuries from overzealous or punitive restraints lead to claims for compensation, and cause employees to be disciplined or dismissed. Personal safety and professional competence may potentially be more compromised by a case of restraint than other interventions, hence the need for clear guidelines of practice, and a policy for implementation.

Restraint is generally accepted as appropriate in order to protect oneself, others' property (to a degree), or the aggressor from self-harm. There are no absolutes, and at present the best guidance is case law. This means that you must be able to justify your actions as reasonable before a court if you use restraint. And your actions must show that you did not increase the violence in any way, say by using excessive force, use of a weapon, or that your restraint was excessive or prolonged.

When restraint is needed only very exceptionally, for example, in a mainstream school, it is best not to attempt it unless absolutely necessary and then only to effect the escape of oneself or others from harm. This pretty much reduces the issue to one of self-defence.

Occurrences of restraint that go wrong can come about because of a variety of problems such as unclear management, too few staff, ill-advised expectations, and an overzealous or angry response driven by a desire to control or punish the other person. Staff will be reluctant to intercede in situations when they might subsequently be accused, and where the support and recording systems are poor. The range of accusations has included unwarranted simple assault, systematic abuse, sexual arousal, and revengefulness. And staff and clients who are anxious about a situation may already be tense, which increases the likelihood of an issue getting out of hand.

Punitive restraints do occur and these beg explanation. They can result from staff venting feelings more properly directed elsewhere, or from inadequate training, or they may be the way the culture of the establishment deals with its transgressors. For your safety, try to foresee any issues that may arise and raise them for discussion or instruction.

Ensure instructions given to you about the use of restraint are unambiguous. Restraint frequently represents a snap decision made in difficult circumstances. If you have to restrain be sure you know what to do, why you are doing it, and that your senior managers will back you up.

Be restrained with restraint.

Section Two:
The Organisational
Environment

Chapter 5

The Physical Environment

The environment must be assessed for risk in particular ways, and then be appropriately controlled in order to meet the needs of clients who may have problems with anger.

Environmental factors are a prime concern of formal risk assessment procedures. It is not intended here to inform on risk assessment processes, but to raise some issues for comparison against the factors considered in the risk assessments you do. The purpose of the establishment will largely determine how relevant environmental issues are, and what form they might be, but risk reduction is always a result of forethought, and is often associated with reducing the environment to minimum essentials. There are two main areas:

1. The Built Environment.
2. The Living Environment.

1. The built environment

The Built Environment is the buildings, fixtures and fittings, including furniture. Risk factors might include the age and design of any buildings or overall campus, suitability for the purpose of accommodating or receiving people who may behave aggressively, and its potential for contributing to safety or otherwise.

Details are related to design, the amount of space, the ease of supervision, absence of blind corners, or poorly lit areas, and things related to the quality, number, and choice of fitments such as the provision of domestic facilities, security of storage, and suitability of furniture.

The following examples illustrate concern with the built environment:

- In an establishment where residents were occasionally violent, a marked reduction in injuries and incidents involving chair throwing was achieved. The chairs were originally the stacking type made of lightweight plastic and steel, and the decision was taken to replace them. New wooden chairs were chosen that, being heavier and being actually much more substantial, were less easy and less spectacular to throw. (Choice of general resources.)

- The use of safety glass in areas where residents have access in a juvenile psychiatric unit. (Appropriate building material.)
- Panic buttons and CCTV at critical locations in a secure home for people with challenging behaviours. (Application of technology following an audit of risk.)

2. The living environment

The Living Environment results from the interrelationship of the built environment with how it is used. Routines and domestic practice used within the particular physical environment will contribute to safety or otherwise. How the environment is managed includes considerations such as density of use, supervision ratios, time given for activities, and how events are organised. Sociometric principles and similar considerations may be relevant to ensure that clients enjoy a safe and satisfactory daily life.

The following examples illustrate concern with living environment factors:

- Magazines were innocently supplied to a young girl in secure accommodation who was then able to self-mutilate by using the metal binding staples. (Suitability of individual provision.)
- A young man suffering from a psychotic episode, and wielding a large chef's knife held a worker hostage for an hour in a stairwell. (Resulting issues were: security of kitchen equipment, and review of surveillance routines.)
- In a large middle school (9–13 years) lunchtime scuffles and fights were frequent at the entrance doors to the dining hall. A consultant determined that the doors should be given discrete uses, and one each designated for school dinners in, packed lunches in, and a common exit. The use of tables was zoned. (Change of routines and use of spaces.)
- In a Young Offenders' Institution, workshop tools are ALWAYS rigorously counted out and back. Tools are normally taken for protection or attack rather than to effect escape. A missing implement will trigger elaborate and thorough search routines that are a bother to staff and inmates. (Implementation of a consistent policy and procedure.)

Control of the environment (20)

If viewed as a technique, control of the environment relates mainly to the living environment, as this is most usually open to more immediate intervention than alteration to the built environment. However, as environmental control for both the living and built forms, is usually obtained by forward planning rather than a response, it is likely to be an outcome of some form of risk assessment whether formalised or not.

A checklist of examples of Built Environment factors that help safety:

- The 'psychology of colour' has been employed, and the décor is fresh and clean.
- Facilities are pleasant and waiting areas are supported: i.e. WCs, baby changing, reading material, toys, refreshment (water dispenser).
- Blue lights in WCs to make it difficult for any intravenous drug users to locate veins.
- Effective vision: i.e. good lighting, sufficient open space in front of reception desks, strategically placed mirrors.
- The area is checked to be free of potential weapons.
- Quiet music.
- Good ambient temperature – maintained even when crowded.
- Supply of fresh air.
- Chance to access a covered outside space (smokers may need this).
- Consulting rooms are big enough and not overheard by waiting clients.
- Reception conversations can be private.
- Informal seating in preference to lines or rows.
- Fixed furniture.
- CCTV is employed and is well sited.

A checklist of examples of Living Environment factors that help safety:
- Positioning is considered in interview rooms and for reception personnel so that escape routes are not blocked.
- Solo visiting is only undertaken following a risk assessment to indicate it is viable.
- Buildings are not locked up by persons alone.
- Report back procedures and mobile phones for peripatetic personnel.
- Personal attack alarms provided (and not left in bags or lockers).
- Alarm buttons, alarm codes, and help points.
- Personal identification badges are removed when off site.
- Zero tolerance policies are displayed.
- Office interviews are preferred to home visits if indicated.
- Client throughput is monitored and staffing levels adjusted to ensure efficient handling without undue delay (may include use of flexitime and review of lunch breaks).
- See also the list given in *Effective Personal Safety*, Chapter 6.

The two areas may be difficult to tease apart. This is illustrated by recent developments in social benefit reception offices where violence to staff has been reduced by the introduction of wider counters, softer lighting, carpeting, and plants (built environment), together with improvements to staffing levels at critical times (living environment).

Control of the environment means consistently implementing the principles of risk reduction. Most workplaces have plenty of opportunity to make improvements; the trick is not only knowing which are the important factors that may make the difference without always having the benefit of hindsight but having an approach to work that supports safe practice.

It is unfair, for example, to thoughtlessly subject vulnerable clients to constant test by exposure to situations they find difficult to ignore. This may happen if desirable possessions are left casually around, or a door is left unlocked. Obviously, possessions that are taken will lead to upsets, but clients may well be very sensitive, and they may make elaborate interpretations particularly when worker behaviour is not normal practice. Tempting items left around may be resisted, but at the cost of increasing the client's anxiety about self-trust, or a client's anger and suspicion may be aroused by their belief that a relationship has tests of trust attached to it. The client may feel unready for this, or find it insulting and react inappropriately, yet the reality is that the temptation results only from a thoughtless act. Putting away bags, keys, food, drink or cigarettes is usually always the best practice, and in larger establishments often normal security policy for theft avoidance. In any institution it is helpful to make it very clear what belongs to you, your client, or the place, and what the rules and expectations are, **for everybody**.

Elizabeth had money taken from her bag she had left unattended in her office. This was in a residential therapeutic community. Only one young person had been around, and staff were certain this particular boy was responsible. However, there was a community meeting scheduled before anyone could make discreet enquiry, and the theft became community knowledge. Elizabeth was well respected and the community expressed strong feelings about the theft. This compounded the guilt felt by the child responsible and created conditions of greater difficulty for the particular child and those who took on resolving the issue.

One effective interpretation of controlling the environment is to restrict choice. Generally the rule is to provide only what is needed, this will control the parameters of a situation. Reducing opportunities for temptation or attraction for impulsive actions will help clients feel secure in a range of environments, and help promote their concepts of self-control and self-discipline. This is most often the safest procedure. It avoids conflict by reducing the stimulus of a wider range of options, which can be too exciting, or too difficult for some clients to cope with. It is rather like not giving a young child a choice of anything in the sweet shop, but offering 'a selection of one'.

A limited environment can make it easier to focus on task – if you want people to cook meat pies, don't put the cherries on the table. This reduction of choice avoids the potential for conflict that can result when 'the chef has to remove the cherries', that is, stopping someone messing with a resource or implement. A resource will also physically last longer, and retain its inherent value for use if access is reasonably controlled. This may be a useful consideration when budgets are under pressure. Familiarity brings contempt or a lack of novelty in its wake, and this reduces value, either for use as a reward, or as an option of choice for clients.

Control also keeps the issue of ownership clearer. Free access can cause a client (and staff on occasion), to begin to feel that they own a particular resource. This is especially so if there is little competition for it, or it is kept a long time. The resource may later have to be removed, restricted, or shared, with consequent possibilities of hurt feelings, or cause for anger. A useful preventative measure is to call in or inspect the resource at regular intervals, even if it is then immediately assigned back.

Inexperienced or inconsiderate workers often overlook the need for a well-controlled environment, and often difficulties or blame is then laid on the client. It can also be important to consider whether particular practice has come about because of concern about clients, or the convenience of staff.

Consideration of the living environment, whatever the setting, is invariably a matter of sensitive evaluation about resources, time, and space. The effect of poor consideration and shallow conclusions can result in undesirable outcomes for clients in wide-ranging circumstances. This is very often the result of insensitive or inexperienced staff practice, rather than deliberate intention to provoke. The following actual occurrences are typical:

- In a nursery, some infants show some aggression to peers because they have to play in a space that is too small, or have too few of the toys that are most popular, and one infant is assertive so that their wants predominate. This particular child is then viewed as **aggressive**.

- A client is approached insistently to do some planning, form filling, or staff 'want a word', but the client is reluctant as they happen to be comfortable in another activity, such as taking part in a game or watching TV. The client is then described as **unco-operative**, and by further insistence is pushed into anger and eventually has to be restrained.

- An issue is raised with a client that creates anxiety in them, but the timing is insensitive, it is just prior to bedtime, or departure for work or school. The client's behaviour is then **disruptive** that night, or at their daytime placement. This is reported and the client's **aggression** is noted without reference to the trigger antecedent.

- Removing a resource such as a TV from a group, although only one resident is suspected of damaging it, **provokes others to anger**.

- A resident is unofficially regularly given access to the kitchen to make late night drinks, but is seldom supervised. The cook reports delicacies missing and no explanation can be found. The resident is not accused, but the next night the care worker withdraws the privilege, and the resident reacts angrily, with the incident reported as **aggression**.

- A plate of scones is provided at teatime for a group of children with behavioural difficulties, but the number needed is made up with a fresh doughnut. No one oversees who gets the doughnut, and a dispute occurs between two children. After intervening, staff reasons the child who is considered **aggressive** was to blame for the dispute.

- During playtime at a very small junior school many of the children (aged 7–11 years) like to play football, but they have to organise this themselves. Supervising teachers do not have the skills or inclination to referee, and disputes are often resolved by kicks and punches, usually from the more dominant older boys who see themselves as expert. When hurt children complain, the school staff intervene and accused children are sent off the yard and viewed as **bullies**. Playing football for a number of children is a balance of desire over the potential for hurt or blame.

- In a nursing home too few staff were available to assist residents at mealtimes, and some of the residents most needy of help had to wait until last before they could be fed. The management approach to the issue was to expect understanding from residents about their staffing problems. Although angry at her treatment at mealtimes, one of the most disabled residents was losing self-esteem and becoming depressed as she worried any complaint from her would be seen as **troublemaking**.

Manage the physical environment effectively. Reduce its potential as an actual source of harm, or a source for conflict.

Controlling the setting (21)

Positive control of organisational factors reduces conflict.

If the physical environment is as safe and organisationally effective as it can be, the next most important factor is to ensure that this is supported by how work is undertaken. Control of the setting is pro-active, and alterations will be an intentional change to organisational structures or routines, and is reliant on interpersonal skills and sensitivity – a form of practical application of emotional intelligence.

The setting for any event or process will contain a wide range of factors that will be within control or influence, and to ensure these do not promote client anger is good practice. Day-to-day considerations may mean sensitive choices about the best places and best moments to do specific work with clients. Longer-term considerations include ensuring that routines and procedures are effective and not counterproductive.

Two key phenomena that create difficulties are 'cog-jams' and 'flashpoints'.

Cog-jams

Cog-jams are people or organisational arrangements that do not work well, and this might be always, or at certain times. Cog-jams are linked to the living environment in that they usually result from ineffective ways of working, or poor procedures. Staff and clients experience the kinds of frustration that end in upset, or the cog-jam provides a focus point sufficiently provocative for feelings already carried to spill over.

Poor efficiency is the most direct cause of cog-jams. This is things such as lost mail, mislaid files, running out of stamps, arriving late, cancelling meetings at the last moment, reports not properly circulated, and inadequate minute taking. Sometimes the frustration continues without change because of operational load, and no one person has the time or the motivation to initiate (or enforce) more desirable practice, or get even simple things done such as an equipment repair. A less direct example is a decision or oversight that causes difficulty made by a colleague or manager too remote to be properly informed or too removed from the consequences; remote may mean from the operational time, the place, or from the people concerned. Too often when the difficulty surfaces it is junior or less experienced colleagues who must resolve it, not the person responsible.

Although they are usually obvious, taking time to review experiences or incident logs will identify cog-jams. Most systems will benefit from some improvement. For example, if the appropriate person cannot answer calls, systems that log the call-back promised, and check that it is done, will considerably assist quality assurance and reduce client frustration. Elsewhere, tasks can be prioritised within a filing or case handling system that shows system status, and individual case positions at a glance. Wall planners are only of benefit when they are actually used to flag up and assist the prioritisation of specific events, in conjunction with location and time diaries to account for the work and whereabouts of staff.

The worst cog-jammers can be senior managers.

> Peter was principal of a very busy residential special school. He had the practice of personally going off-site to do the Cash and Carry shopping on one of his main duty days. This reduced his accessibility to residents and staff, and often problems would be on hold until he returned. Eventually he delegated this task, soon after a decision that he did not like was made in his absence.

It is worthwhile occasionally to audit the actual work and functioning of staff compared to their job descriptions or the model of service organisation, and check that you, your colleague, or senior, are not doing the work of another, or the other way about. It is supportive to all when everyone does what they are paid to do, and that gaps or overloads are identified. It is psychologically healthy to do something about poor systems, or raise issues with colleagues when keys, paperwork, or event changes are not passed on. Don't ignore frustrations.

Avoid cog-jams by anticipating problems, and take precautionary measures. This is very cost-effective when it saves the expense that can result from poor operational planning or non-completion of work. An example of cost-effective cog-jam avoidance is when attendance at an event by all parties is essential, and individual service users, or staff, may need assistance for this; it may mean providing transport or providing an escort.

Remember the pessimist's rule that 'if it can go wrong it will'. Sometimes this might mean it is best to over-provide than chance under-provision, since 'two pints of milk in the fridge' is always better than none.

Flashpoints

Flashpoints differ from cog-jams as they concern particular moments of routine or physical space, and are points when tempers flare because of some inadequacy in people or provisioning. They may well result from a poor quality built environment.

Physical flashpoints are usually easiest to identify and remedy by changing routines or provision. Examples of such problems are a corridor that is too narrow when groups pass, a shortage of easy chairs in a lounge, a door in an awkward place or opening the wrong way. Flashpoints also occur because arrangements favour people with competitive or dominant type behaviours.

People may suffer from an inadequacy of resources or facilities at particular times. Examples are: too few bathrooms and a resident who is always moaned at by peers because of slowness; the distressed client who needs an urgent response, but the system is busy, and they are confronted with a non-prioritising queuing system.

The dining room in a care home was too small for the numbers of residents on those occasions they were all at home. It was difficult for diners to access their tables from the servery. The tables by the servery would be taken up first, there was always a lot of movement, and chairs had to be shuffled about as people squeezed by, and sometimes food would spill. Mealtimes could be quite tense affairs, and tempers would flare quite frequently.

The home decided upon family type serving. A waitress was employed. It invested in serving dishes, which were put out once a table had a full complement of people. Movement was cut dramatically, and everyone liked the new arrangement.

Flashpoints do differ because the tolerance of people differs. Flashpoints can be particular to individuals who confront new circumstances or a change in a personal situation. The flashpoint occurs when a new client (or staff) will not tolerate what everyone else has become complacent about; or new circumstances become no longer tolerable and someone can no longer contain their anger. The outburst is often violent and may seem out of character, but often, poor consultation is to blame.

> Sarah was a resident in a care home. Room changes had to be made that meant she was moved from a quiet location to a room at the front of the premises overlooking a busy road. She was disturbed by the traffic and slept poorly. Sarah had communication difficulties, which contributed to her being seen as compliant and non-assertive, when in fact she was depressed. The situation increased her distress and she attempted suicide early one morning.

Empathic, effective staff will try to preclude such flashpoints by their skill and experience, and the routine use of advocacy and good preparatory communication for processes such as plan reviews. Imagination and empathy can considerably reduce anger or distress.

Changes of personal autonomy are frequently behind a flashpoint event, either as an immediate source or an underlying reason. The loss of autonomy over something important to a client often results in feelings of anger and frustration. These feelings may be expressed immediately by protest or complaint, often about an unrelated trivial issue, or they can emerge later when a circumstance tests the patience or security of the client concerned. Classic examples involve loss. Losses of autonomy include unexpected institutional residency or imprisonment, suffering the imposition of a blanket rule, loss of mobility, bereavement or other loss of a close partner, or of anyone who acted as the client's life broker and advocate.

Conversely, increased autonomy and the reduction of external controls can also create flashpoints. This is illustrated clearly with children, and the flash points of conflict that can result because adult supervision is reduced. It is then that scores can be settled, or bullying occurs. Flashpoints may be represented by lunch and play breaks, by the captive space of a changing room, the bus home, or an unsupervised area.

Effective control of a setting requires sensitivity to the environmental factors. It is important to consider the conditions that ensure privacy, or how to signal seriousness. One of the dynamics is 'territory'. Recent developments in site security of institutions such as schools have established clearer boundaries, or put fences, where previously there has been an open campus. These send a strong psychological signal about territory to people who might enter with anger or dubious intent, and can deter intrusion. Fencing represents an example when the built environment is considered.

Although it can be easier for staff to feel most confident and assertive when their own territory is made explicit, efforts to exert control beyond the boundary may now be less respected. This is an important consideration for many personnel who may wish to influence behaviour or intervene in matters beyond the normal workplace site. I believe it a factor in the unfortunate stabbing of the Head teacher, Phillip Lawrence, in the street outside his school: the street was gang territory, and beyond the 'legitimate' bounds of teacher authority within the school site.

The territory effect operates on venues for meetings. A summons to the boss's office usually indicates a meeting of greater importance than an encounter in the canteen. The psychological effect of setting is taught to salespeople who are trained to overcome the disadvantages of selling in a client's home.

Territory is also signalled by totems or symbols of expertise, for example the way some professional people deck out their offices with credentials. Age, place, personal prejudices, and credentials may all combine. Consider for example how one may feel intimidated taking the car to the tyre fitters. Would you naturally prefer to trust the older mechanic wearing the company coverall, or the younger man in greasy jeans?

It is important to pick territory with care. The setting always carries signals and subtleties. With children, it is normally insensitive and unwise for an adult to violate the safe privacy of bedrooms with a difficult or confrontational issue. It is always better to raise a disciplinary matter in privacy, rather than in front of fellow workmates. The corridor is probably a better place than the classroom to confront a student; particularly so if a loss of face is to be avoided (and especially so if the student is normally a good role model). It is a culturally important consideration with many Afro-Caribbean male adolescents.

Some situations can potentially be very inflammatory. For example, in a residential setting for young people it could be very clumsy to take one person to task on an issue in a communal space with other young people about. This would readily be seen as an affront, and it may provoke an aggressive response as they seek to maintain their standing among peers. Alternatively, with another young person this may reduce their personal and group esteem, or give an excuse for bullying by peers who may think they can take up your issue in their own way.

Set the setting means considering all the dynamics before an action and the action is then taken in conditions that are as controlled as you can make them. This means imagining how others will react to what you set up, and how aggressive responses may be minimised or best responded to.

Think ahead about any setting to make sure you can control it sufficiently to ensure it will work smoothly and safely.

Chapter 6

Health and Safety Matters

Health and safety law

The Heath and Safety Executive (HSE) **regard as violent any incident of verbal abuse or threat to staff, as well as actual assault.** The HSE stance is that **good systems** should be at the forefront of all measures for employee protection.

All employers have a legal Health and Safety duty to protect employees and non-employees 'so far as is reasonably practical' from any work-related violence or threat, and by common law the public from violence or the threat of violence related to the business of the employer, and the employee has a duty 'to take reasonable care for the health and safety of himself and other people who may be affected by his act or omissions at work' (Health and Safety at Work Act, 1974). **This means safety is a responsibility to be shared between employee and employer.**

The law is moving on this point to the extent that there is now legislation under which directors and key employees of companies may be prosecuted for 'corporate manslaughter'. Employees who ignore warnings signs or are complacent about protecting their colleagues can be found culpable of ignoring safety responsibilities. The legislation around negligence, jointly or separately, provides for some very large fines.

There is now also clear case precedent that employers must consider prior experience and training before allocating responsibilities. It is established that it is unfair to put an employee in vulnerable situations without appropriate support or training (Beverley Lancaster v. Birmingham: a junior clerk was transferred to a neighbourhood housing office with no experience or qualifications in that area of work; this led to her eventual breakdown; awarded £67K). And precedent that employers should adequately support workers harmed by violence at work (a former residential social worker from Essex awarded £103,000 by the Criminal Injuries Compensation Board).

If your work brings you into contact with abusive or angry people, or you manage those who do, you may be negligent of your or other's safety if you wait until something happens: **ensure you know what is the policy and procedure for such events.** If there is not clear guidance, ask for it, or provide it if your responsibility. Guidance should normally be part of induction training, and written up in employee handbooks. Additionally, contracts may detail procedures that apply if personnel are at risk of harm, or if they act violently themselves.

It is the statutory duty of employers (Management of Health and Safety at Work Regulations, 1992) to assess health and welfare risks to employees and take practical steps to protect them from reasonably foreseen dangers. RIDDOR 1995 regulations prescribe for 'any act of non-consensual physical violence' done to person at work; and requires a report on any incidents that result in an employee off work for more than three days. This includes emotional stress as well as physical injury, and the legislation is clear that suffering as a victim of violence should never be considered as 'just part of the job'.

Even if the work only occasionally requires managing people who are violent, then appropriate procedures, training, and senior staff support are all reasonable expectations. If an event is a one-off, but proceeded by threats, a series of minor problems, or other antecedents that are worrying, your employer should be informed and expected to respond appropriately. The outcomes of risk assessment concerning conflict can depend on the degree to which incidents of aggressive behaviour occur. But whenever, or however, aggression to staff might happen, the HSE expectation is that employers have appropriate measures in place. This will include some degree of instructions to employees or actual training when appropriate.

The safety of you and other persons can depend on this training and the supporting policy. This means that **risk assessments** are done to evaluate the likelihood of incidents of aggressive behaviour or hazard of physical violence; what its nature is; what can be done to reduce it and the impact of outcomes; and any necessary new measures are implemented. All this must be routinely reviewed and documented, and any changes implemented to update practice by training, instructions, standing procedures, and documented policy.

The HSE expectations for all establishments with *quantifiable risk* **include:**
- a definition of violence
- a statement of principles
- an action plan
  (a prescription for most of the measures below, particularly for a responsible manager and employee support).

The action plan of organisations pro-active on safety will have all the following measures in place:
- A schemata of the preventative measures.
- Guide lines for employees (this may include a policy on internal harassment as well as how to respond to situations with an external source).
- The name of the senior manager responsible (not just the designated post).

- The circumstances when internal 'security' or the police are called.
- A complaints procedure (for employees as well as clients).
- A reporting procedure.
- A support system:
  - immediate response (medical help, place of safety)
  - counselling (debriefs or longer term as appropriate)
  - legal and Representational (rights supported by employer)
- Record and review procedures as part of senior management duties.
- Public or service user information advice.
- Posters (when merited) that inform about the policy on disorder.
- When practical and advisable to do so, a written clause included in service user agreements (with acceptance signed for).
- Line manager on call system of persons who acknowledge the issues and are involved when necessary (immediately and subsequently).

And an organisational culture of no-blame and a non-critical approach to employee distress that will respectfully accord individuals the substance of any experience they report. Alternatively, workplaces where staff become distressed and are not given appropriate support will count the cost in less than best practice, and stress related absenteeism and illness. In the worse scenarios, where employers resist acknowledging difficulties by ignorance or intent, personnel massively lose faith that matters might ever change, and come to believe they cannot themselves have any power to better their situation (the sort of outcome illustrated by the Case Study later in this chapter).

Safe practice

Where a specific policy on violence is warranted, its construction and implementation is obtained by attention to the following operational practice:

- Events inform practice (i.e. it is a learning organisation).
- An outline is maintained of the principal concerns to the organisation regarding violence and aggression (this may be reviewed by audit or other enquiry).
- Normal operating procedures are designed for minimum risk.
- A statement about the normal range of responses, for threats as well as incidents.
- Other risk assessment procedures, when, and how they are to be applied, and the range of possible responses.
- The **threshold point** at which staff should call for collegial or senior support.
- The **threshold point** at which staff should call for, or inform senior managers.

- Line managers with specific H & S responsibilities understand issues and are ready to be involved (issues of training, or 'shop floor experience').

- What part of the policy is communicated to the clients staff work with, and how.

- The allocation of specific responsibilities.

- Ways to ensure appropriate training, and the means to ensure that everyone understands their individual responsibilities.

- Self-protection training (not the same as self-defence training).

- How staff will be protected if attacked.

- How staff who may suffer violence are given after-care support.

- Recording, reporting, and monitoring, and review procedures.

Safe systems

One of the most effective ways to reduce the potential for aggression is that service systems are effective and efficient. No matter how good policy is, or how skilled or well intended employees are; all can be undone by a lousy system.

Systems that minimise client frustration work efficiently as they see it, and will accord them respect in how their situation is evaluated and processed. Services usually have quality standards concerned with keeping service users informed. Quality systems have similar attributes no matter what service they provide. There is little difference in principle between the desirable attributes of staff attitude and operational practice across a range of services, although the methodologies will likely be radically different. Consider as examples this range of scenarios: a child in care (i.e. who may wish to make a complaint) a distressed citizen (i.e. who presents themselves at a local social services office for whatever reason); an adult with learning difficulties (i.e. needing the routines and structures of a day centre); and a college library reception services (serving a range of students). Consultation processes are the most sensitive means for use when checking out objectives associated with quality standards. This is user focused rather than service focused, and may require some shift in attitude and new training emphasis if outcomes obtained are to be of real value.

Transparent reception and client handling systems

The organisation's portals impact immediately and directly on service users. How well reception, caller, and call handling systems work will influence the regard and subsequent expectations of service users. The following bullets illustrate quality attributes:

- Service inquirers are received or acknowledged immediately even if then the system has to 'process them'; and if so, contact is maintained (ideally by the same person).

- There is means to keep users updated on the time scale of process or if there are operational changes by telling them, and use of wait time information, and slips or memos when 'in the system'.

- There is a prioritising option sensitive to user circumstances that can 'fast track' users, or give them additional attention (whatever is appropriate – rather like triage in A&E).

- There are no automatic expectations (i.e. that the user is literate, or will make 'desirable or normal' assumptions).

- The user is given status checks and updates, and these are two-way: information about the service, and check that there is no change to the user's situation.

- If there is service delay or operational change the user is consulted that this does not make a problem (examples: miss the bus home, become too hungry, or generally something else important to the user depends on the service delivery).

Effective administration

Administration impacts primarily on employees. Staff who get the best work done are supported by effective systems that maximise how they feel informed, in control, and safe at their work. The following bullets illustrate the attributes of quality administration:

- Posters or leaflet information is readily displayed or given to clients to inform about quality assurance codes together with a schemata of the service system (names of places and people, the connections, and what happens where).

- When appropriate, prominent and clear display of rules or intolerance notices, disclaimers, action codes, etc.

- New service users on first use of the service or facility, sign an agreement, and are given copy of the pertinent information and conditions they can expect or have agreed to meet themselves.

- The service maximises its use of IT to ensure a quality service and protect staff within provisos of data protection and that any confidentiality issues or special sensitivities users may have are respected, for example:
  - To protect and maintain service quality and ensure there are no *cog-jams* (explained in Chapter 5).
  - To identify clients with a history relevant to their own and staff safety: especially drink, drugs, past threat of aggression.
  - To note another family member's case if it is relevant knowledge (i.e. carer or dependent).
  - To note any known life grievances and recent factors pertinent to the client's own and staff safety (i.e. past poor treatment, loss of job/children/other bereavement, religious or ethnic considerations).

Evaluation mechanisms

The service must have a means to invite report, as this is an invaluable means to inform quality other than inspection processes. Evaluation impacts on employees and service users. It can empower or enfranchise users who are disillusioned but without specific complaint, as well as invite praise that may otherwise go unremarked. Personnel who work for services that are perceived as open to user comment are less likely to be targeted by service users in order to unload frustration or anger. The following bullets illustrate the attributes of quality evaluation:

- The formal complaints procedure is well advertised and easily accessible (and the grievance procedure for organisation personnel):
  - **Complaints are shown to be welcome** and when the origin is open they are acknowledged and thanks are given.
  - Advocacy is provided for service users for whom it is appropriate.

- Suggestion boxes are to hand with slips inviting comment (anonymous or named).

- Audits, or methods such as structured interviews, are used from time to time to sample service effectiveness and user satisfaction.

Effective personnel safety

Services that value their employees will have systems and procedures that support the safety of their personnel. These measures will be preventative and practical. Employees value more the measures that avoid an event occurring than any amount of tea and sympathy afterwards. This means arranging that there is accurate and up-to-date risk-factor information, and speedy back-up or rescue support. The following bullets illustrate effective points or attributes important for personnel safety:

- Who decides whether workers are alone or in pairs or more; and where work is best undertaken(*1).

- Lone workers have personal phones or alarm call facility.

- Internal signal codes are set up which can covertly alert colleagues or security staff when immediate support is needed.

- When appropriate staff off-site are advised to remove any identification badges they normally display.

- The organisation has zero tolerance of abusive and violent behaviour as a norm, this is unambiguous policy and is shown by practice whenever or however necessary(*2). The zero tolerance is contiguous – all personnel are equally supported, no matter who they are within the line structure or where they work.

- Action is evident, and whatever is the appropriate action (i.e. bans, exclusions, or prosecutions) is seen through to conclusion. And this action is publicised by whatever is the best means so that employees know they are protected, and would-be aggressors know such behaviour is not tolerated.

*1. A review of the impact of lone worker procedures found that experienced mental health workers viewed these with mixed feelings, particularly if imposed without sufficient consultation. It was reported workers resented what they saw as intrusions into their professionalism; used by management to monitor movements and workloads, and only with proper impact when there had been an incident. (*Community Care*, 14 March, 2002: 40.)

*2. *Community Care* also found (27 November, 2003) employers did not always provide adequately when social and health workers were blamed by clients for service actions that angered them, particularly when workers were subjected to campaigns of threat and violence by disgruntled clients.

Analysis

Events must not be 'lost'. Best practice is to learn from conflicts by scrutiny of their antecedents and outcomes; effective reporting and review does this. Logs of some sort are essential not only primarily as a record (i.e. for reasons of registration requirement or for litigious possibilities), but because logs can inform practice. Effective recording notes not only the actual instances of physical confrontation, but also the near misses, however minor, and however averted. However, it matters most what is done with the information.

The main tools to analyse physical conflict (indeed all reportable incidents within organisations) are Mapping and Case Analysis.

Mapping requires noting and overlaying the time, place, and other facts related to each conflict event. This may be electronic or paper data. Information can literally be mapped with a plan of the workplace site or schematic of the organisation. Colour or coded marks or pins are used to locate the incidents. Tables or spreadsheets are used to document the moment in time and persons involved. Incident history will develop, and any patterns will emerge as data clusters or peaks to highlight factors that merit consideration. Typical data is:

- the places incidents occur

- the times incidents occur

- the personnel most involved

- the clients or service users involved (by category or individually)

- the people or activity combinations with highest incident

These forms of data analysis provide powerful 'risk assessment' tools as part of the overall assessment strategy and inform operational considerations. They illuminate trends or problem areas, pinpoint factors within the Built and Living environments (see Chapter 5) and indicate where new responses are needed, such as may concern supervision, staffing levels, and training needs. Such analysis helps to ensure organisational effectiveness by monitoring people, routines, facilities, and site: who, when, what, and where.

Case Analysis requires each event be scrutinised for its origins or antecedents, the event deconstructed, and outcomes examined. This needs to be more structured than simply based upon the bare information typically reported (verbally or written). Ideally the senior manager responsible for safety will speak with as many of those involved as possible, and a clear account obtained. Case analysis can reveal cultural mores, and the sensitivity of the organisation will be illustrated by the skills and attitudes of the key personnel concerned. Everyone will benefit from any learning outcomes that can be obtained or from new measures taken. The key questions are:

- What happened before the particular conflict?
  - Were persons already angry or distressed?
- What was the trigger to the particular conflict?
  - What set it going?
- What actually happened (there may be several versions or views that will need resolution)?
- What can be learned about the people involved?
  - Did anyone's actions inflame or quieten the situation?
- What is the 'blame ratio'?
  - How might responsibility or causality be apportioned between particular people, exceptional circumstances, or the system?
  - This is used to inform training or structural review, NOT as means to pin blame on individuals.
- Are changes to systems or personnel advisable, or is some training or other development indicated?

Constant monitoring by mapping and case analysis is absolutely essential in places where violent incidents are routine, as a matter of health and safety requirement. It can show where the flashpoints are (see Chapter 5), and who is increasingly involved in violence, or at risk of it. Inquiry into the near misses can show how events were successfully handled, and which staffs are successful, or otherwise. Obtaining an independently minded 'blame ratio' is a very useful exercise; after all this is exactly what courts do in cases brought before them. All this information is quantifiable in different ways, and will inform about ways to make a safer workplace, or a better service by means such as professional development, or operational change. The following points list the relevant kind of enquiry:

- What kind of violence?
  - To which people, individuals, the self, or a group; property, or both, – slow to rise or spontaneous?
- How severe was this?
  - Compare to norms within and without the setting.
- What were the characteristics?
  - Details about persons: age, background, status (of all parties).
- What were the aims? What was the intention of the violence?
- What was the situation?
  - When and where and for how long?
  - What was the frequency – an isolated/unexpected incident or one of many similar?
- What were the precursors or antecedents?
  - Within a continuity of development or not?
  - If a traceable development, what were the prior relevant indications?
- What outcomes are there?
  - What was the immediate result?
  - What was the effect upon each of the involved parties?
- What new planning is indicated?
  - How might the incident have been prevented?
  - What has been learnt?
  - What might need to change?

The rigour of a system that seeks such full and factual accounts puts stale evaluations to the test, and ensures people do not remain non-questioning and non-questioned. It challenges the relevant institutional and personal systems that may be hung onto for the confirmation of old prejudices or preconceived ideas about violence.

Sick record case study

I was recently engaged to provide an expert witness court report that provided me with case details that illustrate well the characteristics of poor health and safety management and the ignorance of trends. The case concerned an employee who had a nervous breakdown and a collapse of chosen career following a minor assault by a client. This had been preceded by other assaults, periods away from work, and other difficulties for which there had been poor operational recognition, and afterwards little proper support offered such as professional counselling. The workplace was a large local authority institution that has since closed down.

Briefly, the subplot history included loss of staff confidence when the on-site management was disbanded in favour of central control; this resulted in resented decisions and unclear operational responsibilities. The number of aggressive and disruptive incidents increased over several years. There was documented staff concern about this but no evidence of appropriate employer response. However, analysis of the establishment sick record was most telling. It showed a clear trend of increasing sick leave, and indicated a substantial number of injuries that are associated with restraint difficulties. Generally the institution was a very unsafe place (for clients as well as workers). The employer had appraised none of this until mid 1999 when some dramatic changes began (too late for the claimant). The degree of negligence became so apparent as the case mounted, that damages were settled out of court.

One of my charts is reproduced to illustrate how well data informs when it is properly deployed and presented. In this case the rapid rise of sick leave within a particular personnel group, characterised by particular features, in this instance the 'selected' category was ill heath for psychological or mental heath reasons.

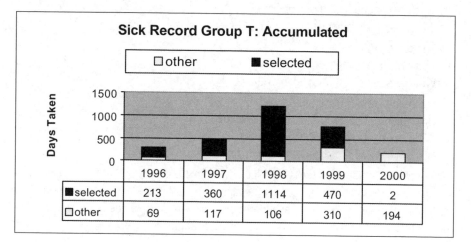

	1996	1997	1998	1999	2000
■selected	213	360	1114	470	2
□other	69	117	106	310	194

Analysis is most beneficial to the people involved. Guilt and blame can swiftly follow violence. Blame is invariably pinned to an individual (colleague or client); and there are links here with the mechanisms of scapegoating (see Chapter 7, Scapegoating). Guilt and self-blame will affect most those who have high levels of conscientiousness.

Consequently, analysis (and responsive supervision methodology) helps reduce unrestrained group or self-apportioning of responsibility, and provides a balance. The proper apportioning of cause and responsibility will best inform about the reality of risk; it is a supportive counter when there is inappropriate self-blame by staff, and it will help dissolve any improper support for a system or a person. It may also ameliorate the responsibility attached to the aggressor.

One of the often-unnoticed consequences of violence to staff can be a reduction in their personal effectiveness. Few other events are so immediately 'person-centred', both when they happen, and by their outcomes. Other incidents at work will have costs, but these are usually to do with money, pressure on the system, or customer satisfaction, thus the outcomes are less personal and consequent feelings less likely to be internalised. Dealing with violence may leave staff fearful of their safety or of mistake, and it frequently leaves staff feeling de-skilled as self-blame causes self-esteem to drop. The person may become more hesitant, or over-reactive.

The vulnerable situations include places where systems and personnel have been in place for a long period without incident, places where the dynamics have been changing but without recognition, places where some common causes that generate aggression are unquestioned, and places where managers escape culpability by pinning blame onto junior staff. All these represent dysfunctional systems or organisations with the potential for worse problems. When the 'weak link' is seen as the worker, despite that the reality is more complex, the person concerned may inappropriately resign, a final form of damage to someone probably already a victim in the situation.

Damage to individuals within a workforce may not always result from scapegoating and collusion, so much as insensitivity, poor understanding, or simply mismanagement. How organisations respond to employees after an incidence of violence is very indicative of their culture.

Effect of violence on the self

Should you or a colleague ever be the victim of violence it is worth recognising the feelings of fear, betrayal and doubt that will prevail.

> *The effects of a violent attack can include nausea, headaches, sleeplessness, shakiness and extreme fatigue, as well as the direct physical injuries sustained. The emotional and psychological impact of violence can be profound and long-term. Common responses include a sense of isolation, and problems in decision making in both personal and professional areas of life. Fear, anger and feelings of revenge, sadness, betrayal and self-doubt all play their part, with one or more of these being more evident at any one time. The fear of further violence, and the lack of confidence in handling potentially violent individuals, can have a serious impact on professional practice. Sudden and unexpected feelings of overwhelming fear are not uncommon.*

Diana Lamplugh and Barbara Pagan, *Personal Safety for Schools*

Victims will have a range of needs. They may need counselling to deal with their feelings, and a sensitive response will arrange for this as well as offer acceptance by listening and by encouraging the victim to offload. They may need to retell the attack repeatedly which can be trying to colleagues, yet discussion and empathy are important to the process of helping the victim accept what has occurred. Time out, perhaps by a change of duties or routines can help confidence to be regained.

Insensitive responses include any criticism of the victim, or implication that they have been unprofessional, and if this is reasoned after an incident that has had its antecedents, why has the manager or supervisor not intervened before? Responsive colleagues and management will be more concerned about pro-actively ensuring there is not a recurrence. This is far more important for safety, and healthier than anguishing or deliberating about what was not done.

If there is not a clear documenting procedure, perhaps because the event is very much an exception, a detailed report must still be made. This can be put into existing records such as the accident record, diary, or daily log. A serious incident must immediately be reported to the local Health and Safety Executive (a national helpline is on 0541 545500). Any accident or violence that results in staff absence from work for three or more consecutive days must be reported within ten days; HSE provide a form for this report.

A worthwhile habit is to keep a personal professional journal or diary in addition to any work records. As well as noting things of personal value, use the journal to note any significant professional matters. Use common sense and intuition; note the date and time of important events or things that you become aware of that worry you. This will include instructions you give, or are given, notes about meetings, snippets of information, and names. A journal like this is invaluable if you need to present, or defend, or raise an issue. There are precedents that such journals can influence court judgement (one famous case vindicated Richard Branson concerning libel about bribery and his interest in the National Lottery).

Chapter 7

Organisational Culture

Professional context

The techniques in Section One centred on communication skills and inter-personal methods of intervention. We must also consider that people as organisational groups behave in a corporate manner, and this behaviour may at times be aggressive, either directly, or through the systems used to deal with service users. This is a matter of organisational culture, and simply meeting legislation guidance or avoiding public concern does not obtain quality. Safe and effective organisations work hard to maintain their corporate ethos by awareness of some subtle factors, examples of which are presented. This is the concern of this chapter, but first you may like to do Activity Two.

Professional review: activity two

The activity evaluates your team or group approach to prime task, in the form of an audit. It may be done alone, with a colleague or with a small group. It may be useful to do this activity in conjunction with a senior or supervising colleague, or be used by them to raise training issues. The task is simple, but may raise issues that will need further resolution, and it is related to activities designed for 'vision forming'.

Allow over an hour (about 10–15 minutes each for stages 1–4, and at least thirty minutes for stage 5), but not considerably longer as a first response will usually represent what underlies the understanding about your work.

Consider the work that you do

1. Write down what you think the objectives are of the project or team or work that you do.
2. Write down what you think is the mission of the larger organisation you work for.
3. What might be damaging or aggressive behaviours or actions of the people you work with?

   What are possible sources?

   Can generalisations be made, or are issues very specific?

What are the main conclusions?

4. If you have done this with others now make comparisons.
   Come to a consensus or rough agreement if you wish.
5. Now determine:
   (a) What comparison is there between 1 and 2? Write down points of high/low correlation.
   (b) What comparison can be made between your notes (from 1, 2, and 3 above), and any documentation such as policy documents and mission statements?
   What correlation is there, are there compromises, if so why and where?
   (c) Triangulation: Compare your notes on 3 with any existing external or fresh viewpoint. This could be an inspection report, or the views of a visiting senior manager, or the views given by experienced staff new to the organisation. Discuss any discrepancies.

Continued inquiry

This may take the form of action research into your workplace. Further analysis might involve describing how the objectives are met, and what resources there are. This may be a list of different people's expertise. Is there a sensible correlation of resources to task?

It may be advisable to do a more inquiring form of audit. Go over the past six–twelve months and assess service delivery. Determine occasions when there were events of aggressive behaviour. This is done by using measurable criteria such as how many cases have been concluded, at what level of time/cost, at what level of conclusion.

More personal inquiry can be made. Ask people what makes them angry related to the work. Clients may be given follow up questionnaires. Colleagues may be interviewed to see to what extent they feel they are able to discharge their professional responsibilities. Question the why, where, when, and how, of the work undertaken. This may also include inquiry into 'things that are not done'. This sort of task can uncover dominant factors, and situations that have been disregarded.

Getting to the core of problems can require great sensitivity and require mediation skills and professional distance in order not to be collusive. A recent example for me concerned my advocacy work for young people. In one particular unit, I began to receive increasing complaint that restraints were too readily used or led to injury. The measure of this was such that I later found that the Social Services Inspectorate had noted similar concern.

My discussions with staff revealed their view that the mix of young people at the time was particularly difficult to manage, and they were without any say regarding new admissions. They were concerned to ensure young people with histories of self-harm and aggression were sufficiently supervised and controlled so that no incident or inter-personal difficulty got out of hand.

I moved from simple empathy with the young people caught in an insensitive environment, to recognising the degree of counter-transference between two sets of people, both 'captive' and facing the same fears and uncertainties about control and safety in the other set.

The underlying adult issues included staff training needs, the number and inexperience of staff at particular times, and a lack of therapeutic supervision in a regime caught between the methodologies needed to maintain safety as well as obtain the trust needed for effective intervention work.

Workplace and espoused theory

Practice and the prevailing ethos is seldom exactly to the letter as written down policy. It may vary from shift to shift and between different teams doing the same work. It could vary considerably from intended purposes and method were it to be accurately analysed. It is to do with the culture you are actually part of compared to what is claimed. It is 'the gap' between organisational mission and achievement.

All organisations make claims or aspire to qualities they do not fully realise. This is not overly significant unless the gap between aspirations and achievement widens to the point it causes service users or organisation members to be dissatisfied. How close this gap is, is a key indicator of total quality management (TQM) principles. This depends on the quality of managers and the degree they are able to distinguish between **espoused theory** and **theory in use**. Understanding this distinction helps people to think analytically and self-critically, to identify the relationships, systems and processes, rather than focus on the superficial or immediate causes of discrete events.

A loss of balance from the compromise of original intentions can affect the most august institutions. A few years ago the FBI found its forensic science procedures criticised; apparently truthful scientific independence has been compromised in a culture dominated by the desire to successfully prosecute principal suspects.

The way groups and institutions work is that aggression is often a subliminal response, represented by ways that are maintained because there are interests at stake such as status, power, or control. Often the aggression is hidden or disguised by restrictive practice for which rationales are held. Or selection procedures are not sufficiently discriminative.

The feminist or ethnic case for equality and recognition has in the past few years included some fire and police services, and the military services. There have recently been some notorious matters that have challenged and exposed a number of organisations and their need to encompass modern values and equal opportunities, many of which have come to light by investigative and undercover reporting for television and the press. Long established and traditional organisations unwilling to embrace change typically become a redoubt for their members. At their worst they are a multi-faceted bastion of culture and tradition, shored up by selfishness, ignorance, fear, and outright prejudice.

The pathology of all organisations is expressed in how its people work together, and how closely the qualities that drive their mutuality also direct the way service users are treated. This is another area where any organisational 'gap' is undesirable.

Workforce culture

People are seldom completely alone. Your personal effectiveness depends to a large degree upon the mindset of colleagues in your workplace whatever the degree to which you have freedoms compared to given parameters in which to work. Remember also that 'what gets passed down gets passed around'. This tends to be true whatever the trait, particularly passing on blame, bad-mouth gossip, and some forms of harassment.

When a group is led by one dominant person it is tautological to point out that the ethos of the group will follow the style of its leader. This may be a caring and nurturing environment, although that is more often found in situations where the hierarchical structure is tempered by notions of equality. In other situations comparisons may be imagined where the senior manager in a workplace may operate much as a lad of fifteen might bully and dominate a gang. Both will cause the culture they impart to gain ground if they are in a position of influence and remain unchecked. The victim stereotypes are wimps or women, and the work stereotype hard and male.

The truth is that victims are much more universally found. Not long ago Bedfordshire and Cambridgeshire Councils had to investigate allegations of bullying related to management styles. This sort of 'white collar' harassment is often difficult to pin down, and it will be masked in onerous or unfair rotas, reports that are binned, put-downs using wit or sarcasm, or a clique that keeps the victim on the outside.

If you are victimised or harassed at work there is help available. The first port of call will be your union or professional organisation, and most now have dedicated support for members so troubled. Other organisations produce guidelines, or will help put you in touch with local support. These are listed under Contact Information at the back of this book.

With work place aggression it is not always easy to see who the victims are, or how they suffer, or recognise how and why the aggression is manifested. This depends on factors like personality, age, sex, the degree of isolation, or on opportunity. People who are put upon may try to disguise their discomfort in front of their colleagues or supervisor as they may not want to lose face, or they believe that others cope with what they cannot.

Conversely, they may be provoked into open and hostile response, or secret sabotage and destruction. When problems are internalised, they may cause depression or engender feelings of low self-worth. If this is you, get help. This may mean finding a way of opening something up for discussion, or seeking advice from a support organisation, such as from a trades union, or seeking help through the contact list. If you see this in others, help them.

Client assurance

A useful way to ensure service users experience quality treatment is to compare the three 'C's' of culture' against quality assurance criteria. The three 'C's are:

Consultation   Communication   Confidence

When these are given consistent high regard, the relationship organisations have with service users is protected, and potential difficulties are considerably lessened.

Consultation

How well service users or clients feel respected:

- Clients are made to feel welcome and invited.
- Reception staff are trained how to receive clients who phone or call in person – including if they are distressed or angry.
- Reception areas are comfortable, and there are playthings to keep any young children amused.
- Reception privacy if at all appropriate is always maintained.
- Clients do not find assumptions are made about their understanding of service matters.
- Clients find that staff do not use jargon when talking to them.
- When appropriate clients are:
  - invited to contribute
  - informed of their rights
  - offered advocacy
- No action is taken on behalf of a client without it being fully discussed and not against their wishes (even when possible for exceptional matters of legal responsibility such as Child Protection).
- Lay members or service user groups are accorded respect, and their representation and wider communication is supported.

Communication

Service users or clients are given clear information as appropriate, which may include:

- Brochures and guides.
- Names of personnel and their responsibilities.
- Contact numbers for messages and/or direct contact times.

- Being kept informed of any arrangement alterations.
- Being regularly invited to raise any issues they may have.
- Being provided with contact information for any support organisations they may be interested in.
- Consultations are scheduled when possible sensitive to other pressures on clients.
- Consultations once arranged are protected.
- Consultation privacy is ensured.

Confidence

Some key considerations about personnel that assist service users to have confidence in them, mean that personnel:

- Are sensitive to the possibility that some clients will have bad recollections of previous or allied services.
- Understand that clients will not all be equally literate or have English as their first language.
- Do not let issues develop to any degree of concern without intervention.
- Always do what they say they will.
- Are always well informed about what they may do and are honest in their undertakings.

The cultural constructs

The following six constructs raise awareness about some less obvious – often unrecognised – ways that group or organisational culture might be aggressively dysfunctional.

Nicknames (1)

Surely it must be a happy bunch of people when everyone has a nickname? Possibly, but very probably not.

A nickname is shorthand – a handle onto a person, giving instant identity. Nicknames are often found in groups and in fiction, and in these contexts they work well providing all that is wanted from an individual is that they fulfil a role, and that is all that the 'character' has to do, whether real or fictional. Significantly, groups where death may suddenly occur invariably make much use of nicknames, such as army units in action.

A nickname alludes to a role or some aspect of character that denies the fullness of individuality. It is a caricature. The stereotyping effect can be very moulding. Conversely it can be used positively to build up self-concepts, as in calling the cook a chef (or equally that example is used with sarcastic intent). Used positively these strokes can be very ego building to persons with poor self-esteem, providing they do not set up expectations that cannot be met.

Because nicknames stereotype and devalue the individual they are seldom determined for their positive benefits, which is why they should be avoided, and people usually prosper better without them. They can represent a covert form of aggression, and be intended to upset or anger the recipient.

Nicknames underpin fixed images, and the perception of others that is unfortunately difficult to break free from. Those who try may be put down as unsporting or 'uptight'. They may encounter strong and antagonistic resistance, a saint may wish to be a sinner (or the other way about) but no one will allow it. People put others down because of their need to maintain their place in a pecking order; and giving derogative nicknames to others helps them do this. It is a significant indicator of power imbalance if one person refers to another by a nickname, or by first name, but in return will only accept being called by a title or proper name.

The use of a Christian or first name is similarly a sensitive issue, particularly if the person has no say in the matter. This may be because there has been a shift of power balance or autonomy (see Chapter 5, Flashpoints), or it is a cultural consideration. Sometimes a small matter to others has larger significance to the subject. This was illustrated to me upon meeting an elderly resident in a care home who felt angry that care workers used her first name without her permission. Behind this lay the feelings that her care workers were too familiar and disrespectful.

In a similar fashion name diminutives can carry a negative image. Recently, a developmentally immature young boy, Jamie, that I had been working with had friendship difficulties, he always seemed to need to prove himself at the expense of others. He had also been considering how he would cope with the transfer from a small primary to a secondary school. In conversation he suddenly volunteered: 'and I will want to be called James'.

Look hard and long at any nicknames you encounter, and determine if they should be used. Here are three examples of worthy people I have come across where nicknames were used to meet the needs of others, and helped to deny the truer person:

- A very caring man working within a residential institution came to be called 'Fat Wallet' (this at the time of the Access card TV advertisements). The man was big and enjoyed his food. Residents out with him could be sure that if they ate out it would be at the maximum cost expenses allowed. The nickname actually implied easy access to food, as well as a rather cruel finger-point at the man's physique. Use of the nickname by the residents was hypocritical of them, but also indicated some despising of a man easily used by them because of his preferences. It took him a long time to shake free of the nickname and its connotations.
- A team was joined by a very skilled therapist, who competently filled a gap in their work, but he did not have the same sort of qualification as the other team members

and he was also the youngest, although at most by only a year or two. He came to be known as 'the lad'. Although the team liked him immensely and accorded him considerable respect for his work, full membership was just that tiny bit denied, subconsciously I think, by use of the nickname. The therapist would often challenge the team about their treatment model.

- A very caring senior supervisor was known behind her back as Peggy. The workplace did not encourage much in the way of support to junior staff, and the culture was rather cold and macho. Younger employees quickly learnt to be hard-nosed and act as if they did not need any support, and so they followed the line of keeping Peggy at a distance, and this was made easier if Peggy was known by her nickname. Peggy, whose heart was real enough, actually had an artificial leg.

An analysis of any nicknames used among the people you work with may be very revealing in what it could suggest about your workplace interpersonal relationships, about the prevailing attitudes towards clients, and about the psychological health of you all as a group. Anything with racial or sexual connotations is of course completely unacceptable.

Using nicknames is demeaning to both parties, and denies people their individuality.

Scapegoating (2)

Scapegoating has a strong link with nicknaming in that it indicates similar dysfunction of interpersonal relationships. The scapegoat is useful to others for the feelings of superiority they can extract from having a scapegoat around, so that the spotlight of criticism is not on them. Or, a scapegoat acting as a point of focus for a lot of bad feelings or difficulty helps others forget or ignore where the real problems are. At its simplest this is 'a kick the cat' sort of syndrome or the way some partnerships try to deal with their mutual acrimony. The partnership dispute can be played out by large organisations.

I was once involved in a situation concerning the placement of Kenny, a very disturbed and acting out teenager developmentally stuck at an earlier stage of tantrums and phobia, and often confused about what he wanted, like a small child torn between sleep and excitement. The social services department involved became at odds with Treetops, an independent residential facility, where they had placed Kenny.

The SSD had limited resources of its own, gave mixed messages about the referral, and was uncertain about Kenny's needs, which was showed by inconsistencies in their casework. Later it was unable to find a respite for Treetops when it came to a point where Kenny and Treetops both needed this. The SSD team manager began to question the ability and resolve of Treetops, and whether Treetops understood Kenny's needs, and refused to fund any respite (a scenario that many social workers will be familiar with).

The SSD shortcomings were belittled by Treetops from the start of placement. Treetops suffered in part from some smugness of culture. The fact that they took on particularly difficult children that others had often refused, gave rise to some arrogance in the face of criticism, rather than any admission that there might be children beyond their 'saving', or so damaged that their needs might never be adequately redressed. The pair of establishments, through their principal officers, came to quarrelling like a pair of rejecting parents. All this delayed dealing with the real issue, albeit painful, of Kenny's difficult behaviour, and he became more out of control and more violent.

Within groups, typically the scapegoat is castigated for a perceived personality trait, inefficiency, or a personal difference. The scapegoat is kept on the fringes of involvement, and sometimes misdirected or under informed for the vicarious pleasure got from their failure. This makes an issue that the rest of the group can share and so they feel better bonded. Scapegoats lose self-esteem and confidence, and with anxiety may actually make mistakes, which further compounds their position. Examples are the boy who always seems to be to blame for playtime scraps, the junior manager who is never efficient enough.

Sometimes the only way scapegoats can fight back is by being what they are accused of, and they commit small secret acts of sabotage and revenge, mail is delayed or 'lost', or keys thrown away. The 'smelly' child will defecate on the cloakroom floor.

Scapegoats can be difficult to spot either because everybody agrees on where the blame lies and there is a massive collusion to maintain this, or because the scapegoat has fallen into a role and to an outsider it seems they do all that they are accused of. It can be both, it depends how independently you acquire your viewpoint.

Scapegoats can be subject to so much venom that they escape. They leave or run away. Sometimes they can become completely rejected by the group that gave rise to them, and another will be found. In a group made powerful by common ties and under threat by the need to change, a scapegoat may be made of the team leader who tries to introduce developments.

Groups who are under pressure to make change may not be able to discuss this openly, especially if the change implies some criticism of existing practice. The group may begin to tighten up, become collusive, and find a mutual tie by focusing on something external to them. Usually this tie is nothing to do with improving the quality of work, but it may be a form of power struggle. Roughly expressed the group faces change or die, but it believes that it will die if it changes. The common tie will not be a collaboration of quality; it will be collusion within a dichotomy.

John began to wonder if he'd made the best career move ....

During the past few years a number of schools have amalgamated. Often the preparatory work was not sufficient to properly assist the people concerned to anticipate positive outcomes, nor were the practicalities of amalgamation well orchestrated. Consequently, many of these schools have had staff groups in difficulties, which could be seen to fit the dichotomy model. The typical pattern associated with poor school amalgamation illustrates well how a dichotomy model might operate:

Two groups, staff teams from the amalgamated schools, are forced into a merger. The new group remains divided and weak, as it is not forged together by sufficient shared vision and purpose. The new school struggles along rather ineffectively until a scapegoat is found. This allows the group not to take responsibility for their failings, but it does unite them. The scapegoat may be the Head teacher, after all, they have probably been the one person who has tried to remain impartial, and maintain a dialogue with both subgroups. The situation worsens and the Head then resigns. The staff group have now more or less completely withdrawn from accepting responsibility and making any 'collaboration of quality'. The school is failing, it becomes a news item, and the news focus highlights the number of 'unteachable' children (new scapegoats). The Local Authority Education Department then comes under scrutiny and is found not to have given sufficient advice and support in the past (much the situation at The Ridings School).

Senior managers would improve the success of their ventures and limit better the potential for damage if among their ranks were those who understood well the mechanisms of interpersonal dynamics and how the health of corporate pathology is achieved and maintained. Too often decisions that backfire have been driven only by political plan and accounting considerations about resources.

It is important that every professional person has some understanding of scapegoating processes. They will then be more able to guard against being caught up in a dysfunctional situation. A major risk for many workers is that they may carry blame for an aggressive incident – particularly if it has bad outcomes.

When there has been a violent incident the worker may come away carrying personal feelings of remorse and inadequacy. This is especially so if it involves a client they have previously been working with successfully. The worker will question his or her own expertise and responses. This makes for a set of psychological preconditions that make scapegoating that worker an easy option. A good supervising colleague will talk all this through and arrive at a realistic evaluation. What must be avoided is personal blame for inadequacy because of lack of training and experience. Frequently an incident has more issues than the adequacy of one person.

There are attitudes that help create scapegoats. A typical attitude is denying a problem and creating isolation for the scapegoated person. This shows by comments such as, '*You are the only one complaining, no-one else has a problem with X*'. Some attitudes attempt to lay blame, this will show in more sneering comments such as, '*I don't understand, no other warder has your problems on B wing, you must be soft in the head or the arm!*'.

For some managers it can be easier to lay the blame on the unfortunate worker rather than face up to issues of service or staffing inadequacy, or of their own mismanagement. Do not create a scapegoat, do not allow yourself to become one.

Scapegoating is finding someone to blame other than self and avoids dealing with issues properly.

Collusion (3)

Collusion is a very insidious disturbance of organisational pathology. All sorts of groups, but particularly closed societies, can manifest this sort of behaviour, from couples to townships. A great deal of fictional literature has been based on the phenomena and the consequences or outcomes. There is always a pay-off. There is always something deliberately or conveniently ignored. There are always victims.

The pay-off can be cash, perhaps something like a deliberate system or pretence of ignorance about expenses claims. Or the pay-off can be in reinforcement of thought, as in, 'We are the best'. In both instances the pay-off here is inclusion within a group. A group can be a very powerful block to development. Collusion has links with the kind of stereotyping that supports nicknames, and links with the process of scapegoating, and with pigeon-holing.

Pigeon-holing is when a group has such a fixed perception of a person or an issue, that all its interactions become so reinforcing that the concepts are seldom challenged, thus all observations are made to correspond and are immediately 'pigeon-holed'. When a sequence of people begin to share a perception it is most comfortable to be in agreement, and it is difficult to stand aside and submit a different perspective.

The common perspective also has an influence on what you might otherwise think, when ideas, words, and thoughts are presented to mould your thinking and be echoed in your vocabulary. The 'halo' then helps maintain inertia of consideration, and something or someone will continue to be labelled, although closer analysis, or subsequent behaviour, might support this even less. This halo effect can produce heroes or scapegoats. It is the reason why the best formal reports, about ideas, or on people, are gathered independently or in camera, and not collected on a circulated form, or from a gathering. For example, it can be very difficult for an individual to vote independently when there is the traditional show of hands at union meetings.

A good way to avoid collusion is to be wary of professional jargon. The shorthand this represents can preclude objective consideration, and is a means to maintain power. In a meeting or in reports it can exclude the non-professionals, or allow those on the inside to rapidly be presented with a stereotype or a solution that forestalls further deliberation. In a conflict situation with a non-professional it can fan anger by excluding the aggrieved person.

A common collusion is to do nothing, but pretend that existing practice is good. It's called 'follow the system'. This means fill in a report, do what is normally done, pass the file up, or down the line, and is also known as 'refer and forget'. Sometimes people are overstretched, and more work may mean less is done well, or it will increase stress factors, consequently refer and forget helps to keep things manageable. It can come about through too much burden as well as indifference or laziness. Ultimately refer and forget has its cost, and invariably this is represented by clients disillusioned, frustrated, and angry about the delayed response, and their marginalisation.

Often collusion comes about quite innocently simply because no-one steps back to look at practice.

> In an institution dealing with challenging behaviour a visiting Registration Inspector made an analysis of the incident log. The name of one member of staff, Jo, cropped up time and again on entries concerned with restraint. Although only a few residents spoke disparagingly about Jo, at first the obvious interpretation was that she was out of step with colleagues with indications for some need of training.

ary and complaints procedure that should be part of your contract, and
by step in professional dispute with your employers. Although this may
to cover their tracks, it can be a way of forcing to the fore issues that
and ultimately, if you come before an industrial tribunal for resolution,
for your concerns. My experience is that persons chairing industrial
sensitively to the individual employee in this position.
ngerous form of group dysfunction: understand it.

n is always valuable, yet it can become lost as the daily demands of
from maintaining a healthy perspective upon what they do. Different
alities also contribute to how a matter may be viewed. Clients and
ge over time, but there is often a time lag before the service responds.
ns and roles may be useful.
ly quite static formal expectations on expertise or how a job is to be
tions include matters like a daily report to a senior manager,
th and Safety checks, the ability to drive, and good primary care
ate the organisation framework. They will be represented across job
e management structure, and all the functions are normally covered
mplement of staff. Typically, functions do not vary much over time,
neralities they may be found replicated in similar institutions.
asks that people become associated with, and as practice develops
Usually these result from the particular personality or attributes of
y be from circumstances that emerge – people like Jo (see Collusion,
es of the things for which individual people become relied upon
pport, advice, mechanical or electrical expertise, ability with
the ear of a senior manager, public or press relations. Roles may
and go, but individuals may find they have too many roles in small
are personnel shortages. Roles are acceptable unless they hinder
he individual's prime task or restrict the proper responsibility of

ck if there is good balance between your Roles and your Function
wo lists. Under Function note the tasks you do that are a formal
e as Job Description), and the time they occupy. Under Roles note
nd the time they occupy. Is the balance acceptable?
to ensure that the relationship between role and function does
st people can assume roles within a healthy organisation. These
d by the management. Organisations become unhealthy when

Closer investigation revealed someone whose restraint practice was excellent in
method and appropriate on occasion, but the staffing rota placed Jo with one or two
colleagues who were possibly lazy, and several colleagues who were less physically
strong and less experienced. This meant that Jo was doing all the restraint work.

This gave Jo a lot of self-esteem and made her feel important. Other colleagues,
including managers, felt secure when Jo was about and supported the collusion. Jo
was used to bolster up weaknesses within the team and counterbalance the lack of
expertise on her shift. The practice made unfair, and possibly dangerous, expectations
on Jo, and was cramping her professional self-perceptions. It prevented other
colleagues from gaining appropriate experience and confidence, and it was beginning
to have an effect on Jo's relationships with residents.

One of the worst collusions is when practice or individual actions towards clients is punitive
or abusive. In this situation the collusion can be along a continuum. At one extreme it may
be a closed practice that is tacitly acknowledged within, but not shown to outsiders;
families with abusive members can be like this

The middle position has collusion in a suspicion that many harbour but no one dare speak
about. This is because asking questions and opening up the situation may put jobs and the
good bits of practice at risk.

The least obvious collusion occurs almost subconsciously among people. Practice may
continue unchanged, as there are no mechanisms or forces for inquiry. This may be because
of the lacklustre of people involved, and inertia or laziness, or result from a common lack
of experience, or the domination of people by a theory or a person.

I once visited a residential special school that later became known for the sexual abuse
the principal was perpetrating on the residents. The relationships between the young
residents seemed mainly based on power and status, and all my instincts told me the
place was unhealthy, but at the time I could not see beyond the evident power
structures. Discussion with the staff was difficult, as they seemed unable to engage
ideas beyond the problems of daily matters.

Collusion on a grand scale will produce a very static organisation with very closed ranks (see
this chapter, Balance). Some widespread collusions result from the combination of a number
of factors. Officials may at first deny allegations, perhaps these seem too preposterous or
difficult to deal with, or the complainant is not believed. The allegation may threaten to
besmirch a service or the official's colleagues. There may not be any clear machinery to deal
with an emerging problem, or there may not be good interdepartmental liaison.

One of the early findings of the North Wales inquiry (Waterhouse) into the abuse of young people in institutional care was that there had been reluctance by public authorities to act upon earlier recommendations, citing bureaucratic inertia among SSD officers, councillors and the police. The inquiry found reports had been suppressed for fear of embarrassment and compensation claims.

People who become aware of the collusion they are part of have some difficult decisions ahead. They are very probably in process and may be making rapid self-discovery as they become released from old perceptions, and so they are changing. They probably cannot stay where they are as it will become too costly to maintain personal integrity, and new visions will cause them to clash with the status quo. As Shaef describes:

> As people get healthier, they are no longer able to support the level of pathology that is present in their workplace. One of two things usually happens.
>
> As the individuals get healthier than the system in which they work, they either leave and start their own entrepreneurial efforts or they get fired. They cannot stay and remain sober, and the workplace cannot tolerate persons who no longer support the pathology of the organisation. In addition, recovery often brings about a real systems clash within individuals, within families, within organisations, and within societal systems. The recovering person has to move on and keep growing. Non-recovering systems seek to maintain the status quo as a closed system: they are static.
>
> Anne Wilson Schaef, *Beyond Therapy, Beyond Science*

When a conscientious worker from within the organisation confronts collusion, they will encounter severe problems. This may include actual harassment and workplace bullying. This will be either because others do not want them to raise issues, for all sorts of reasons, or as a form of retaliation. Protest may cause them to be excluded from the group in some way, including withholding information and work sabotage. They may be dismissed on the pretext of a disciplinary or procedural issue. Often the grounds for dismissal result from events that have gone wrong because the individual's response did not comply with the norm. Managers can then interpret this as a breakdown of trust and loyalty.

It is critically important to recognise the degree to which the conscientious worker may be at risk following their stance. They may have to contend with their own frustration and intense sense of injustice. This may result in a physical outburst of anger, which would be detrimental to their case. A way of channelling feelings and to protect against being a potential scapegoat is to whistle-blow. This also may be the best thing to do on behalf of service users.

However, be warned that whistleblowers are met with responses such as hostility, embarrassment, complacency, and denial. They seldom retain their jobs; reports by the *Community Care* publication during 1996–7 showed no whistleblowers in the caring professions then had remained in post. The Public Interest and Disclosure Act (1999) was intended to safeguard whistleblowers by providing protection and outlawing gagging

clauses in employment contracts. The Act
victimised if they speak out about malpr
compensation claims, there are concerns it
there has been a breakdown in employer-

Alison Taylor is now well known as the
reported:

> . . . one senior manager visited all
> investigation with a pack of lies . . .
> a devastating experience. My career
> for my family, for the distress they

If you are in a similar position seek help
Contacts section at the back of this bo

Advice on 'whistle blowing'*

Whistleblowers must be prepared t
in the mire, or get out. If you stay, ke
and continue normally only until you
this you will very likely be discredite

Get what evidence you can to su
photocopy logs if you need this
material. Buy a mini-recorder and k
report writing or whatever, but ir
place of safety.

Consider getting union suppor
back to your workplace through
if they are either part of the pro
structure. Try to find out who a
evidence, but be very circumspe
have been in your position and

If you whistle-blow go as h
concern. If careers or instituti
county, or national level, but
retain a copy of your paperwo
substance of concern. Do not

The alternatives are to re
registration or inspecting ro

*Comment acknowledged by

invoke the discipli
place yourself step
give someone time
have been fudged,
it is a public foru
tribunals will respo

Collusion is a d

Balance (4)

A sense of proportio
work prevent people
situations and perso
their needs may chan
An analysis of functi

Functions are usua
done. Typical illustra
responsibility for Hea
practice. Functions cre
descriptions and the li
when there is a full co
and they share such g

Roles are unwritten
and changes over time.
individuals, but they ma
above). Typical example
include sympathetic s
particular clients, having
be fluid as people come
organisations, or if there
organisational function,
others.

An effective way to ch
is to make and compare
part of your job (should b
the other things you do a

The essential balance is
not become distorted. Mo
will be overt and recognis

roles overtake formal functions because the structure has become outdated, dysfunctional, or usurped by collusion. Losing balance about priorities can lead to conflict:

In one particular children's home, keys became the source of considerable conflict between children and residential care workers. The culture was considerably awry in that good care practice had been usurped by considerations about control and discipline. Many staff unfortunately developed the habit of displaying keys by attaching them to belts or little chains, and this drew attention to them, thus keys became established as badges of authority. They then became desirable targets for mischievous and delinquent behaviour from the children. Keys were always an issue, whether lost, lent or stolen. The keys served as a focus for interpersonal difficulties. Many of these difficulties obscured the fact that the proper function of the care staff had become compromised.

Elsewhere, priorities may be controversial or not fully debated; people often resist change. Power can be wielded from peculiar corners, like the ogre caretaker whose cleaning routine determines office accessibility. More usually a practice continues because no one questions a method or routine whose origins are lost in the past. An example of organisational inertia, supported by elements of collusion and by bullying was experienced by Reg.

Reg worked in an office where once a year annual returns from nearly eight hundred satellite establishments were checked out for accounting errors or any fraud. The sums involved were small but the organisation prided itself on tidy bookkeeping, and was dealing with public money, (this is as simply as the situation can be put, and it dates from before computers were in general use, and long before quality control practice). Reg and his colleagues got a considerable amount of overtime work during this period, and the completion of the task was an important moment for the line manager as the returns were used to predict the coming year.

Reg found the overtime work easy but boring, and although a junior employee he was curious. On further investigation he found that the overtime cost far outweighed the sum of errors that were discovered, and the errors invariably cancelled each other out. He reasoned it would be more efficient to accept the returns as given except for some random spot-checks. Reg suggested this when invited to a department meeting.

The line manager found the suggestion threatened his supremacy over the procedure, and threatened his importance. He quickly complicated the issues and squashed the suggestion. Later he raised some antagonism towards Reg from peers whom he alarmed by alerting them to the possibility of losing overtime money. Reg left the organisation which itself much later folded up.

It can be quite a common occurrence for people to become trapped in carrying out instructions that are a source of anxiety to them or simply a waste of their time. They may not be confident about questioning a line manager for fear of rebuttal or ridicule, or there is no mechanism to debate or challenge normal proceedings and cultural mores. Sometimes seeing something through to the end actually becomes the objective.

Do you remember the film Clockwise, with John Cleese in his role as the manic clock-watching headmaster? All too often real people do have a preoccupation with a specific issue or a target that can lead to a disproportionate use of energy and resources. Always keep in mind what are the intended outcomes of a particular course and be prepared to abandon it if it looks to become too costly. Beware the vested interests of others, and watch that you or others are not put upon because of someone else's pet concern.

One of the most stressful situations for a professional is to be so severely constrained by time or money that their integrity is compromised, or they fail to achieve their objectives. Often service limitations will be tolerated until an issue becomes a point of focus that results in an angry reaction, this may be unfairly directed at clients or personnel.

Bullying can develop as subtle forms of abuse because colleagues want compliance. Some workers may feel a bit uncomfortable, but it is not always easy to see abuse for what it is when it is disguised in manipulations, or presented as a reward system. For example the residents in some homes may be very trying in their behaviour, and easy to polarise as a problem bunch of people. Elder abuse has its origins in this kind of dynamic. Shouting at residents, undue roughness, or more subtle control in the form of power over money, visits, and treats, are all ways that can sneak up on teams and become normal methods for them. Balance is obscured when people and systems are hidden within the walls of an institution; this was a feature in the childcare 'pin down' scandal in Staffordshire.

Often the quality of balance is determined by a personal agenda. This may be yours, your colleagues, or belong to the manager. Often it is an issue, perhaps about equal opportunity, or a style of doing things. Perhaps a manager has a very pronounced viewpoint, and everyone may try to be very politically correct even if this has dubious benefits for the service. An aggressive personality style in a supervisor may make workers obliging at the expense of real issues, and this is how much bullying at work starts.

Conversely, actual decision-making often needs firm resolve; sometimes only a manager has this. People may have been running around showing, and thinking how caring and wonderful they are, but not enough gets done because needs exist that cannot be met. It is difficult to prioritise when working with people. Managers also often have the difficult task of intervening in a cosy relationship that has developed, and determining new expectations.

Sally was working as a field care assistant. She was assigned to Irma who as a care leaver needed support to survive in the community because of difficulties related to autistic type behaviour. Sally formed a friendship with Irma and found shared interests that obscured her objective assessment of Irma's needs. Irma held back from becoming too independent, and Sally's supervisor did not use a good enough means to properly assess and monitor her progress, consequently Irma's support was considerably extended. A new supervisor was appointed, and soon after a phase out plan was requested by him.

The new supervisor was at first seen as antagonistic to the team by the challenge he posed to Sally and similar existing poor practice. An attempt was made to brand him as aggressive, and the team became very clannish. Eventually their better reason responded following the interpersonal skill and good sense of the new supervisor. Happily both the professional esteem and the case turnover of the team improved.

A good way to check on balance is by inviting secondments and seeking these occasionally for oneself. These need not be in exactly the same area of work, and ideally are not simply a visit, better at least a week as new learning, or an insight into methods, best develops following sufficiently close acquaintance. Ask the questions and make the comparisons. Another way is to use consultants; like going for a health check.

No guide can teach sensitivity. This means things like how well the situation of others is understood, and the degree of empathy for this. It helps to use imagination, and to swap role or function.

Acknowledging the pressure people may feel can be revealing. For example, a client may present a worry about a peripheral issue; say travelling alone, when actually they have more general concerns for self because they are now looking after themselves.

Testing the balance by some form of audit or searching question is always revealing. Descriptors that objectively report on service quality can determine any gaps between what is intended and what is actually achieved. This will reveal situations that are unhealthy, exploitative or inappropriate, but have not been called into question or recognised. Invariably if something goes horribly wrong before there is redress, there will be an outcry, and with hindsight everyone gets 20:20 vision. This is often a risk assessment issue. The trick is to always seek this quality of vision, and have the systems, record keeping, and personnel to support it, as, for example, ensuring workers are not sent alone to visit potentially dangerous clients, and perhaps meet their death.

Two recent events illustrate the hindsight phenomenon. Firstly, wisdom after an allegation of a specific incident, like the young English 'nanny' in North America who was accused of killing a baby in her charge by shaking or dashing it down. Of course she was initially demonised, but wiser voices then asked how responsible, and penny-pinching, are parents that put young and inexperienced girls in charge of babies and young children, something natural mothers do not always cope with well without support.

The second example is of policymaking that ignored worries. 'Care in the Community' led to many people leaving sheltered or secure institutional care as these were closed down during the 1980s. This included people with learning and behaviour disorders, or mental health problems. As a result there was a significant rise in the number of personal carers and the ordinary public who were killed by their charges. There is now strong recognition that many clients inappropriately had lifestyle changes thrust upon them. They lost medication supervision, or were prone to anxiety and depression following the change in their environment, and their vulnerability increased. This policy was implemented, even though many professionals protested that clients not consulted and put to new and unprepared stress would increase the risk of their aggression.

The best balance is to question even normal practice regularly, and to cultivate the ability to step back and try to see a situation for what it really is or may become. Always be discriminatory in analysis, avoid the cop out of scapegoating, and in determining any fault, weigh up the cause and responsibilities fairly. This is particularly valuable as a way of investigating occurrences of aggressive behaviour, and to avoid circumstances that may make people angry.

Relevant queries include:

- Are there vested interests?
- What are the intended outcomes?
- What are the assumptions?
- Are there alternative viewpoints?
- Are those involved impartial?
- Are the clients satisfied?
- What has worked best?
- Could something work better?
- Are there new wisdoms to be found?

It is essential to continually check that a viewpoint or practice is not stale, and your sense of proportion is valid.

Pathology and style (5)

Cultural style can be a guide to possible sources of aggression. One pointer to a dysfunctional system is when a remote or more senior decision maker unexpectedly overturns operational autonomy; and the worker in the field is either disempowered or compromised as their actions are made impotent. When remote decisions concern young people they are seldom tolerant to changes of agreement, and more likely to respond with acting out behaviour. It is seldom the actual decision maker who then has to cope with the outcomes.

Freddy was fifteen and locked up on remand in a secure unit. While waiting for court appearances, and with charges that were being dropped one by one, he became depressed and anxious. However, his behaviour stabilised, and mutual trust was gained with the staff at the unit. Over several months Freddy worked towards being granted some mobility, short escorted outings that are normal procedure. This helped lift him out of depression. At a planning review meeting he asked for mobility to begin, and was supported in this by the unit staff. His social worker could see the sense of this, consent was given, and the planning detail made.

A week later Freddy's mobility was countermanded. The order came from the senior manager with the social services responsible for Freddy. As the result of an unrelated event several hundred miles away this Local Authority suddenly became sensitive to press reports concerning its children in public care. Worries about children absconding had led to a blanket policy for remanded children. When Freddy's arrangements were taken away he lost his control, and let out his anger explosively against his surroundings.

The people within them shape organisations, and individual personality becomes bound up in the way the organisation presents itself. The two become intricately one. Management theory is used to describe why differences in organisation exist. One theory suggests four pathological divisions (after G Jones, Henley Management College); these carry no comparative evaluation, but serve different purposes and exhibit different styles.

Communal cultures

Communal cultures attract people who are passionate, creative and liberal. They are egalitarian and may support people who are not contributing, but equally, someone who wishes to lead strongly will be resisted. They may have a philosophy that is valued above achievement. They usually have humanitarian aims, and may carry on with a mission even in considerable adversity. Some of the experimental schools of the 1970s might fit here, as do co-operative ventures, and environmental organisations. The only intended aggression is when beliefs have to be defended, but individuals may be sacrificed for the common good, although they will be anguished over.

Networked culture

A Networked culture is informal and flexible. People value helpfulness and trust, but usually have a weather eye open for new winds. Position and work is dependent on keeping a high profile of contact with others. Some very modern commercial organisations are most like this, typically so are consultancy groups, geographically dispersed organisations like a group of professional services, and some charitable institutions. Senior officers within local and national government departments can interact like this when multi-agency work is well developed. An individual who does not fit will be quietly ostracised rather than attacked.

Fragmented culture

The Fragmented culture is normally not well represented by organisational structure. This culture may only exist to serve the interest of the one or two high-flyers who try to retain control. Those people who do well attract others as well as resources, but are frightened of losing their position, this encourages selfishness, and a pecking order mentality. Some research organisations are like this, as well as training and academic accreditation systems based on competing agencies. Individuals may use aggressive tactics to maintain their position, but these will be covert to disguise their true nature or intent.

Mercenary culture

The Mercenary culture is the one most concerned about money or dominance. It is based on measurable outcomes of product or throughput. It will measure these obsessively, and parade standards and performance schedules. The work will be task-orientated and competitive. Dissenting views are not tolerated and people have to work together as expected to maintain results, rather than for any benefit of co-operation or inquiry. Yardsticks are used so that employees or divisions may be measured, and poor performers are castigated or cast out. The culture is characterised by the expectation that constituent parts will be self-financing. Some would argue that the English education system is suffering from the imposition of this style.

Problems arise when people do not recognise the features of the culture they are interacting with or are part of. It can lead to very dysfunctional situations when there is a strong mismatch between organisational culture and personal beliefs. Good observation, analysis, and maybe some intuition can guide judgement about the underlying pathology; all of this relies on adequate information. Consequently, most people are wary to some degree about new positions. What people first see is surface style. They will also be trying to avoid some of the problems outlined already in this section.

The importance of judgement in new situations is because people are often made angry when they become caught up in a system that is not working well, or they feel they have been duped into making a commitment that they find does not suit them. This is true for employees and clients. There are a lot of situations like this, for example, the purchase of services from a new provider, a change of carer for a vulnerable person, a career move, or redeployment.

Although the biggest area of worker risk is a new post, difficulties may well be greater if they only emerge some way into a commitment. There are a number of considerations that can help guide decisions about committing to new organisations and new places, and help to avoid the possibility of compromise. Truly effective and healthy organisations will not usually be let down or dominated by one of its components. Everyone will appear happy in the part they play and all will share a common understanding that shapes efficiency, approach, and purpose, even allowing for different styles and personalities. There is balance and proportion. For example successes are properly accredited and celebrated, and one failure is not unduly damming.

Look to see if everything about the organisation seems well integrated, it usually goes hand in hand with quality, and there will be just appraisal for all employees, and ways of quiet introspection that check that workers and clients are satisfied. If there are very dominant features, are they healthy? Many organisations work well because of strong or charismatic leadership, but such regimes do not suit everybody. Equally recognise that many failing institutions begin to fail from the top down.

The surface style may be interpreted for the supporting pathology. This may be seen in the people, for example by their interpersonal style. Does the manager have a Mutt and Jeff routine with his deputy? Is your reception flustered, or off-hand and not properly catered for? What can be seen by routines and the provision, for example, of furnishings? Are the standards consistent, or is there a huge difference between the accommodation provided for residents, for staff, and for the manager. Sometimes indicators for organisational culture can be seen pretty quickly.

During the first minutes of an inspection of a care home for the elderly it was noted that the manager always spoke of residents as 'they': i.e. 'they don't like . . .' and 'they are usually . . .' Subsequently, the care home was seen as quite regimented. It was not that the quality of care was materially poor, quite the contrary. But there was little to mark the individuality of the residents, and how their individual preferences or needs were acknowledged. Much of the approach and daily routine could be seen as being in place for the benefit of those running the home, rather than the residents.

This regime actually seemed to suit most residents, but one or two others were less happy. A placement consideration at that home would crucially need to consider the degree to which the potential resident wished to retain their independence and valued surroundings and treatment that would be respectful of their individuality.

The pathology of all organisations has some key indicators in the way people relate to each other.

Observation about personnel could include these considerations:

- How are visitors treated: are they shown the cloakroom and offered refreshment?
- Passing in corridors: do juniors or ancillaries say hello and offer a smile, or duck and shoot by?
- Are the women, or the men, fully integrated, or is there a divide due to service and role differences, or perhaps resulting from more subtle and less defensible reasons?
- The way people are spoken about. Is there 'them and us' polarisation? Are residents or clients spoken about as individuals or lumped together as 'they'?

Observation about the organisation could include these considerations:

- What seems to be important, process or product? And what is the place of features such as performance targets, arrest rates, length of stay, costs, client satisfaction?
- What do staff describe? What is the quality of features such as: head office support, training, staff turnover, resources?
- Staffing levels. Do these seem to be minimal, or are there sufficient, or good, arrangements on hand to deal with times when there is crisis or conflict?
- Is line supervision clear, and working satisfactorily?
- Is the building and its rooms cared for, are notices all current?
- Does everybody have a pleasant demeanour, and does this seem to be normal, or do you feel there is best behaviour on show, or crack-papering cover-up?

Observation about cultural mores could include considerations such as:

- What form is the culture? Machismo, resigned patience, service at any cost, caring but realistic?
- Do people behave in a dominant manner with clients?
- Is there a race, gender and age mix?
- Is equal opportunities only a token nod to a policy, or taken seriously as a driving philosophy?

Much of what you might observe on a first visit may be superficial, but determine what it might indicate. Equally at a more subconscious level your intuition will be working, learn to tap into it.

Recently, I had to make judgements of this kind, and was reminded that the size of an organisation provides no certainty that it will be well managed.

The Social Services Department of a local authority had been experiencing a very negative press following a care scandal. The Authority began to try to redress perceptions and a new director was appointed. It successfully bid for government funds to build a prestigious and expensive new facility. This attracted a lot of interest and a complete team of staff had to be appointed and trained.

This looked exciting and I obtained an invitation to a presentation. Many people interested in a possible appointment had come some distance. On arrival I found the reception was confused and confusing, in part because people from several different disciplines were neither separated nor presented with a common introduction. A display had been set up which was not very informative. Some 'information desks' were manned and others not, and the officers were not properly identified.

A dozen or so others and I determined we particularly needed to see one man, but he arrived late. We were not seated and no introductory words were given, the man perched on a table edge and offered a protracted question and answer session that had no structure, and which was further confused by repeat questions as people came and went and generally milled about. At this point I reasoned that if this chaos represented the first stage of selection process, there had been inadequate vision, and lack of clarity about objectives.

Nevertheless I remained, as I knew I had a lot to offer at the training and team construction stage, as well as eventual service delivery. I was later invited for interviews for two different posts, although in both cases I was unsuccessful, and the interviews were not enjoyed. I was only half-hearted, and the experience was marred by limitations to properly engage. The procedures seemed too rigid, and in one instance a planned session, an attempt to implement Warner Report recommendations, was abandoned leaving an unfilled void.

The elaboration of this example is because it illustrates how at the outset I sensed there were difficulties, although I did not actually withdraw. In the event, although I was sorry not to have had the chance to show my strengths, I was glad not to be involved, it may have proved very frustrating. The enterprise seemed to lack effective steering by either a project manager or a strong interdepartmental team. Subsequently, I heard the new facility had significant problems with recruitment, with the choice of personnel, and with operations that resulted in strong client dissatisfaction. Something not begun well is an uphill task.

For the benefit of your workplace and your career, cultivate the ability to view a day as if it is your first, and critically 'visit' your own place of work occasionally, learn to trust your instincts, hone your observations, and marry them with analysis.

Observation of surface style can indicate underlying pathology, experience and insight will inform about organisational culture.

Letting time work (6)

One of the most stressful things is to be put under time pressure. This can create anxiety to make the right decision or to concur with others. People may resent the pressure then, or later, and respond angrily. They may find they have made the wrong decision and will be angry with the person who demanded their quick response.

All managers are usually under some pressure to produce results, or to trim budgets. Some workplaces have an ethos based on a quick throughput. This may be couched as a business-like approach in the degree to which workers are expected to have an aggressive thrust towards dealing with the workload. Watch that the pressures do not become a too onerous pressure on self. Work which may suffer through lack of foresight, or from poor consideration of service limitations, may be better served by more paced consideration. The biggest problem with time pressure is that panic solutions often come undone, and produce more work to do in the long term. Ultimately this can badly affect the quality of a service and the sanity of the people trying to deliver it. Being constantly under time pressure can be an indicator that a manager, or oneself, cannot prioritise well, and probably works inefficiently.

Sally was PA to a boss who could not prioritise. She tried to remain at her job because she was experienced and had a considerable interest in the client group being served. But she was never sufficiently in control of her work, or sure when her day would end. Typically, letters to be done were given to her last thing in the day. Her manager would fuss in and out of her office on petty errands, and gave Sally tasks she would have started earlier had she been given them. He would arrive in a flap because he had visitors he had forgotten he had invited, and Sally had to drop what she was about. He rarely properly delegated effectively.

Although her boss was considerate in other ways, he could not trust his own efficiency so neither could he trust others, and was always inappropriately checking her work. Try as she could to improve communication and manage her boss better she could not impact upon his ways. Sally found her work was invariably too frustrating, or not appreciated. Unable to show her anger directly, or confront her boss constructively, Sally too often left for home at the day's end crying, and depressed. Eventually she left.

Pressure may have to be resisted from clients who are aggressive. They often demand instant response, and present all sorts of reasons for this, or threaten what will happen if their demands are not met. Threats may have served them well in the past to ensure they did get what they want. Giving in immediately will only increase their dominance and decrease your effectiveness, but instant denial of their request may provoke more anger. The best response is to delay the matter, probably by use of one or more of the techniques given in Section One. This will allow you to make a considered response, and give them time to make the realisation that maybe things will not go as they wish.

There are usually gains if time is given in most situations. Giving time avoids knee-jerk responses if action not reaction is wanted. When someone is pushed hard for a decision that is difficult to make, the demand can feel like aggression. If people are forced which way to decide they may then feel victimised, their self-esteem will fall, and they may blame themselves for not resisting, in all a pretty unhealthy situation. Although giving time sometimes allows people making decisions to come to a contrary resolve, at least this is a more sure and honest situation. Conversely, the same resolve can be supportive as time allows the subconscious to work, and for conflicting feelings to even out.

I once had the onerous task of asking everyone on the payroll of an institution to accept a 10 per cent pay cut, including myself. This was one measure I wanted to implement to stave off a looming crisis that I had inherited and in a situation where generally I had good support from colleagues. First I used the 'grapevine' to alert colleagues about the consideration, and I spoke to some key colleagues about the issues. This allowed for the shock response to be avoided and people had some time to consider and discuss among themselves, and with their families.

A few days later I took each member of staff aside and put the situation to them individually. I explained that it would not be imposed and only implemented if there was sufficient support. I was asked what would happen if the measure was not well enough supported and I had to honestly reply that I could only make decisions when situations were certainties. I gave out formal letters, which detailed the main issues and the hopes for reinstatement, together with a reply slip.

In the event only one person, Dave, felt unable to accept the request, and he had said that this would probably be the situation. Dave was good enough to come and tell me this was the case. I thanked him for his forthrightness and I accepted his decision and wanted no rationales for it. I reminded Dave that the outcomes of the canvass would only be known to me and that I would make arrangements so that his decision would both remain private knowledge, and honoured should the measure proceed. A few days later Dave asked to see me, as he wanted to accept the pay cut and do his part in support of all.

Controlling time helps manage pressure. It is often wise not to give or expect 'immediate' responses; this form of pressure can be construed as aggressive, or if couched in dubious rationales is covertly aggressive. This is particularly so in group situations such as meetings. There may be other issues you cannot easily raise immediately, and a blanket refusal might embarrass or anger a colleague. Ready agreement, or refusal, might risk you or the other person with some loss of face, and a quick decision might make for more difficulty if you want to recant later. Pressure can be resisted by a polite and considered comment perhaps along the lines that a suggestion seems OK, but you'd like to be sure you can do things well and need to consider before deciding.

Deferring decisions even for a short while allows matters to be gathered and weighed. Alternatively a provisional but private decision held until your deadline, resolves your inner pressure, and still allows opportunity for fresh considerations. These forms of 'time out' also allow the subconscious to work, and thoughts to form that were not immediately accessible. Time pressure is debilitating, and resisting it when appropriate to do so – even if only for a very short while – is a sound way to assert your self-care. Doing this makes it less likely that commitments are given to a path that is later regretted or resented. Regrets are debilitating – take time over decisions.

Chapter 8

Personal Health

These last few constructs are to do with you. They are techniques and sensitivities I have learnt for myself, sometimes painfully, or I have absorbed from others. The concern is about personal balance, and perhaps if you have not done this before, this may be a starting point for you. To know how psychologically healthy you are is essential before you might question the make-up of the organisation you are in.

If there is a good correlation between your concerns for action, and the expectations placed on you by the organisation you work for then all will be well. The culture of your organisation will be healthy. If you enjoy confidence and ease in a situation it will mean that you will let colleagues know how you are. When concerns are accepted or responded to sensitively, this is a good way for your organisation to develop. If this is your situation you are fortunate.

If this is not the case, is there is a mismatch, do you need to improve your powers of discrimination, are you ahead, or out of step with those around you? These last few pages will not equip you with Teflon skin. Moral responsibility is not obtained by a non-stick cloak of imperviousness, but neither is a coat of Velcro advisable. Valued colleagues do not have an aggressive manner, nor are they persons who attract aggressiveness from others.

If you wish to progress any concerns, either about yourself or work, and you expect a difficult passage, approach it in a considered manner. Effectiveness is about essential personal balance between your needs and your work, a balance between sensitive listening and observing, and the responding skills of selectivity and judgement.

The personal constructs

The next six constructs provide ways when cultivated in self that help ensure aggressive or dysfunctional personal manner does not develop or remain unrecognised.

Silence and paraphrasing (7)

Talk less, and you will hear, see, and understand more. Generally this is the only way to add to the totality of what you already know. Information is going to come from what others say to you; therefore to receive more you will need to transmit less. If you keep the flow up it will be at the expense of your sensitivity. Too often people are wary of silence and are only at ease when conversation is flowing. Beware someone's anxiety does not fill the gap between words.

Silence is a counselling tool in that it is what the other person has to say that is important. Too many questions or too much comment can overly direct the flow of thought, or subvert it as the other person either resists or gives way to dominance, or senses they are not listened to. Silence should be comfortable between friends, and is the skill that makes listening possible.

Silence is often perceived as uncomfortable; particularly perhaps in team meetings, someone will fill the vacuum. Often decisions and suggestions come only from a few of the participants, or there is a palpable pressure to decide. In these situations slowing down or reducing the dominance of some members can allow space for others to add thought, and for better decision-making. You might wish to consider how you compare here. However you might be seen as silently aggressive, disapproving, or withdrawn if too noncommittal, so complete non-comment needs to be countered by your general demeanour of being relaxed and interested. Make encouraging use of nods, lean forwards to show concentration, use 'ums' and 'I see' and 'and?'.

If you lead interviews, case planning or similar meetings providing a moment of silence is especially useful. It can be helpful to suggest a few moments of thought. Often it is only then that someone will raise an issue that would otherwise have not been aired. Pregnant pauses give birth.

Paraphrasing is another counselling technique and part of what you might use in acceptance strategy (Chapter 3). Repeat simply what has been said, this is accepting and invites further comment or elaboration. Do not cap the account by yours, which goes one better or worse.

Put at its most simple, if you love the sound of your own voice go on stage, don't work with people. To get along with and be seen as friendly and approachable, by clients and colleagues, cultivate the habit of using ears and eyes, before mouth.

> From dawn to dusk
> Spending the day
> Gathering clay;
> Surely Buddha would not
> Think this a trifling matter.
>
> From *Lotus Moon*. The poetry of the Buddhist nun Rengetsu.

Personal tranquillity promotes receptivity.
Project self less to understand others better.

Watch your step (8)

I wish I had the gift to see, myself, as others see me. (Apologies to Burns.)

Another important way you should self-monitor is how others might perceive you by your voice and manner. This is the language you use, the expressions and tone, as well as the way you put yourself across in stance and gesture. This is much more than this guide can fully detail, and where ideas like 'Transactional Analysis' and 'Body Language' are applicable (Harris, 1995, and Pease, 1995). Have you ever seen yourself on video? If not, it is an experience worth seeking out, as you will wonder who it is on screen.

> I have a face, which is often very set and serious; apparently it is linked to my brain. I never knew how much people who did not know me well thought I was unapproachable, although I thought myself otherwise. Eventually I was told this by a mature student who came to know me while engaged on research at my workplace, and I am ever grateful she had the courage and the consideration to tell me.

Remember that aggression is often an outcome of anxiety. How do you respond to denial or challenging personal moments, or to thoughts that continually dog you? It may be that in some situations your words and manner are more abrasive and confrontational than you believe, or would want. Either your worry is displaced but it has found someone it can readily be discharged onto, or the situation brings to a head a concern you have been carrying.

Typical situations are not always to do with responding to client behaviour, they might equally be when confronting a colleague or a superior about an issue, or how you deal with some ribbing, or peer pressure. I do not think any adult has not come away from situations that, in afterthought, they have wished they had used a different tone, or put something differently. It can too often seem difficult to find the right tone between wheedling and demanding say, classically, when asking for a pay rise. The solution to all these difficulties lies in confidence about your case whether this is for client or self. Proper self-assertion can be helped by a dry practice run, get a friend to role-play the boss, or the needling colleague.

Be sure you understand well how you communicate your feelings to others by unconscious manner and what is shown by your body language. Control of how you present yourself can help you avoid inviting the wrong perceptions or giving away an inner feeling that you would prefer to keep that way.

Body language can also be used intentionally as a tool to help you communicate yourself to clients, colleagues, and managers. Professional people concerned about their interpersonal communication and body language should be able to self-monitor or arrange for a suitable course. Mirrors, and speaking aloud to self are useful here.

Sometimes it is the most intentionally caring people who give offence. They assume too much familiarity and do not always ask to sit, or they make others uncomfortable by being too close to their personal space. A person may be too 'touchy-feely' in inappropriate situations. Conversely, another may not even tender the warmth of human touch when support or sincerity call for it.

Similarly there are status, age, and cultural variations that impact on how to make good communication. For example, the alienation of black male youth might be reduced if more white authority figures would learn to be less confrontational and 'in your face' when dealing with issues of choice, progress, and discipline. Body positioning can communicate intentions very powerfully.

> A ticket collector was suspicious of a small group of youths who alighted from a train. He took up the 'Headmaster Stance' and stood with chest out and arms akimbo, legs apart, straddling the exit. The youths approached, then suddenly charged him and he received considerable injury, including several broken ribs.

Upright stances may look and feel as if they are controlling, but they are very confrontational. They may compromise personal safety since a good deal of the body kept front on means the other person may more easily jab, kick, or push. A rigid stance does not allow you to easily flex or duck away, and it can symbolise personal rigidity. Courses in body awareness, self-defence and about physical restraint will all cover training points in this area.

> Part of my work at one time was to supervise an area used by teenage boys who occasionally threatened violence. I eventually found a helpful body stance that initially took a lot of self-control. The usual advice is probably to remain on your feet. Many men fall into the trap of squaring up, or at least blocking passage as did the ticket collector.
>
> First I learnt to put my hands in my pockets and perhaps lean on a wall. This seemed better than pacing about nervously. I could still quickly intervene with words or action, but it signalled being relaxed and not ready to attack, as it is non-confrontational body language. Later I began to sit if possible, and invite any person who I was concerned about to sit by me. Sometimes I would draw attention to this: 'Look, I'm not going anywhere. I'm sitting here because I'm waiting for you to tell me what the trouble is properly – so that I can make sense of it . . .'

Choosing to stay meant that the young person was already making choices rather than a reaction. It did not always work, but the benefits for personal dignity, for both parties, and the potential for less confrontational resolutions, far outweighed the consequences of more aggressively policing the area.

A sensitive professional manner will mean that normally, any authority in a situation is not welded in a very overt or aggressive manner. The voice can be softened by the careful use of language, and a permission seeking approach, such as 'May I ask a question about . . .'

Using permission-gathering terms is non-confrontational and less likely to provoke an angered response from a client. This means using opening phrases such as: 'May I . . .?' and 'Is it OK if . . .?' and 'Would it be alright for . . .?'.

With language it is helpful to be discriminating about meaning and for this to show by the words chosen. There is a difference between 'can do' and 'will do' with answers, and 'could you' and 'would you' with requests. The latter form is so much more positive, as can means possible, not necessarily an agreement to action.

Negative language examples:	Positive language examples:
I can't . . . You should . . .	I won't . . . You will . . .
I think that . . .	I know that . . .
I'll try to . . .	Next time I . . .
If . . .	When . . .
I wish you . . .	I don't like it when . . . I want you to . . .

Precision with words underlines expectation, or intent. An idle threat, or an irresolute expectation, devalues the position of the person communicating. This can lead to frustrations that may be resolved by resorting to a sudden and arbitrary intervention, and a conflict is created. Anxiety often lies behind a lack of clarity, and can equally affect the professional as well as the client. Avoid waffle and half-heartedness.

Avoid phrases like:

'I hope I . . .'
'It might be better if . . .'
'I'm not sure, but . . .'
'Do you think you could . . .'
'If this goes on I think I . . .'

A confident person will demonstrate their confidence by voice tone, and the content of what they say. People who nag and whine signal a lack of self-confidence and uncertain authority. They are usually part of a spiral of non-compliance that makes easier the other's predisposition for complaint or refusal, and the issues are less likely to be addressed by other means.

Avoid repetition. In many situations a repeat demand soon after the first can be felt as nagging. If there is non-compliance ask the other person why this is. Ask it and expect an answer, be genuine in your enquiry appropriate to the situation. Watch you do not further nag with whines of the 'why don't you do it?' kind.

Awareness of how you are seen by others, and sensitivity to their response, is an essential professional skill. This includes both manner of voice and physical demeanour. Awareness is achieved by inviting feedback from colleagues or attending appropriate training, and using recording equipment can be helpful.

The skill in being assertive without aggression must be continuous. It is important to present the same self whether championing an issue on behalf of yourself or clients. An important consideration is that employers or others concerned about any aggression in an employee cannot raise the matter easily as it could be contentious. This makes it a relevant issue for supervision discussion, or if appropriate further personal development help. Training is usually available, Community Education classes on Assertion Training may be offered at your local FE College. There are books on the subject.

Cultivate presentational self-awareness.

How you present yourself is a form of sensitivity to others.

Self-monitoring (9)

Most professional people will have some experience of providing supervision or keeping an informal eye on the general well-being of a client or a junior colleague. It is important that this process is also maintained in the self. Keeping a watchful eye on self, in effect self-supervision, will benefit you, your career, colleagues, and clients. People who work well for others also care for self. Not every one understands this, or knows how to obtain it professionally.

There is an important correlation to maintain. To work well on behalf of others, a professional person must have a number of attributes that apply to the self that are the same as those they may be helping their clients to gain. These are attributes such as emotional stability, self-assurance and self-esteem, reasonable physical health, a positive personality, a reliable and consistent attitude to tasks and honesty and trustworthiness.

Interest in the self requires that people come to know themselves well. This is done by maintaining an awareness of the effect of work and life upon the self, and this is what is meant by self-monitoring.

There are several important areas for self-monitoring:

Tolerance thresholds

A self-monitoring check that is always useful is, are your words or action considered; and not reaction. When response to problems is reactive, and with less consideration than normal for you, it shows that you are under stress, and seeking to deal with things quickly to get them out of the way. You will make snappy, poor decisions. Tolerance thresholds are indicated by the degree to which you can normally contend with problems such as noise or interruption.

Thresholds become breached when demand or pressure increases. The pressures may be handling a caseload that is growing too big, or from working too many hours, or other pressures with more personal origins. Your tolerance thresholds will be different from those of your colleagues, and will vary, dependant upon other factors such as your degree of experience or expertise, and how tired you are at that particular period.

It is important to know what your normal tolerance threshold is for one set of circumstances, this is your personal base line. Accept it for where it is and do not allow others to make critical and unsupportive comparisons, especially if this threshold drops away. Try to see what is the true cause of any tolerance shortfall and do something about it.

Personality

Check that you remain 'in character'. Anxiety is a common cause of altered behaviour. It has links with your tolerance threshold in feeling unable to cope with the amount of work, or unable to cope with specific parts. For example, meetings begin to seem more difficult, or now make you nervous. Certain events may precipitate physical symptoms like palpitations.

A main objective of self-monitoring is to reduce your incidences of anxiety. This is because of the links between anxiety and aggression, and depression. Your temperament may change. It is important to monitor this and seek help, or otherwise respond to your needs, to reduce the risk of contributing to a conflict or becoming depressed.

Conversely, you may become foolhardy and impetuous with lost sensitivity. Not putting things off might present as a more positive approach to task, but might also mean more conflict. Change may include uncharacteristic short temper, having a bullish attitude, or a tendency to be very critical and blaming of others. You may feel mild paranoia about the demands made upon you by your supervisor or clients.

Others may also view the bustle one sometimes makes in order to get through work as aggressive and demanding. The person becomes too intent, and without their usual humour. Unfortunately, it is the most conscientious workers who are the least willing to divert or offload their commitments when it becomes too much. And the people most at risk of conflict can be those most anxious to maintain good service. These conscientious workers are also most at risk of transference because they use their emotions to power their work.

Transferences

Transference is the phenomenon where you imbue another person subconsciously with associations rightly belonging to someone else (or they you). This can be emotion loosely or immediately carried over as a mood or reaction that properly belongs in the past or properly directed to someone else completely. The phenomenon is commonplace within the caring professions because the work often causes own emotions to be heightened, subconsciously or otherwise, and often an emotion will sneak up unexpectedly and cross into an area that at first does not appear connected.

Transference can be triggered by almost any association, even style of dress, phraseology or accent. This evokes an emotional or feeling 'memory'. Transference can have positive or negative effect – for example the immediate way it is possible to like another person – or otherwise – without knowing exactly why. Common transferences include the range of emotions associated with the early stages of bereavement, such as denial, anger, and depression. If your working day includes dealing with a lot of hostility or suppressing your own anger then be aware that this may surface and be inappropriately directed later, perhaps a flash temper with your partner for some minor thing.

Counter-Transference is the phenomenon to be more wary of, but it is very useful when recognised. Anyone who has counselling training and experience will have met, under-stood, and used its affect. It means the other person's emotional state becomes the way you feel because of the way they behave or what they say given the dynamics between you. The feelings get transferred to you, and you focus them back. If you can recognise the emotion as it develops this is a very helpful clue to the real source of the other person's feelings although how these show on the surface is different. For example you may feel frustration with someone, but they may appear to be angry, or sulking. Behaviour that is often counter-transferred includes: blame, obstruction or stubbornness, prevarication, humiliation or personal insults, and domination (can have a sexual element). The trick is to take what you feel and acknowledge it, comment openly, but avoid being reactive or laying blame. Say something like:

I'm feeling very frustrated. Despite you shouting at me, I guess that's how you must be feeling if . . . Can we . . .

Look, your comment is insulting – it's stopping me thinking. Please stop so that I can help you best – we both need to think clearly if we are to find a solution.

I'm finding it hard to not be angry with you. Does the way you're behaving mean you're angry with me (or with the service)? How about we both ease up and try to sort this out . . .

A personal example was to experience distress when I had completed a period of successful training and staff support work with a particular team of people. I should have felt satisfied and pleased. I immediately thought I had over-identified and over-associated; this was true, but it was only later that I realised that the parting had caused some feelings about bereavement to surface.

Health

Your physical health is linked to the amount of psychological and physical energy your work demands of you. Stress reduces the strength of the immune system, and you will be more prone to colds and infections. You will take longer to get better.

Watch out for the physiological signs of stress and tension. This will show in things like a tense jaw or shoulders, or the bunching of fists, and loss of self-awareness about physical needs. Carrying such strains for long will lead to physiological outcomes such as back and muscle pain, headaches or poor digestion, and the psychological co-morbidity of depression or cardiovascular problems.

I once had a crisis to contend with, and I'd been away for several days renegotiating contracts with service users. I was driving home when the traffic slowed outside a cafe; it was three-thirty in the afternoon. The smell of food made me realise how hungry I was – I had not eaten since five o'clock the previous evening.

Assertiveness

To be effective for your organisation you need to be effective for yourself, and find a balance between assertiveness and compliance. The demands faced can make life seem like a dilemma. If you give in you feel like a dogsbody, and you will come to resent your situation. If you refuse you risk being branded as unco-operative. This sort of pressure can make a person's words and stance seem aggressive as they defend their position, and will make their intentions more difficult. Assertiveness for professionals means proper negotiation before they are pushed to their personal limits, and aggression and counter-attack is all that is left. If self-assertion is needed, present the case of your workload rather than your feelings, and let the facts stand for themselves.

Even people who are most accomplished at self-monitoring can have problems. Although you may have a balance you invariably maintain, there are times when everybody else seems to outmanoeuvre you. Clients and boss come with demands you can't meet. Colleagues have a caseload that outnumbers yours, and they tell you so!

Another survival trick is negotiation. Delay, by playing for time, or using a get-out. For example, deal with pressures by saying you will have to consult with colleagues or your manager before you can give a definite response. If you have to say no, return with an offer of something else, and preface this with co-operative comments such as: 'I'm sorry I couldn't do . . . I've looked again at my diary and it is just not possible, but I know you are concerned about . . . I will be seeing . . . Would you like me to . . .?'.

This kind of response keeps you in control, and the offer returns the upper hand to you. This way you keep your self-respect as well as winning points for being considerate.

Formal supervision

Many readers will have some form of regular professional management. If this is not so, seeking to have this provided may be an important first step towards resolving the conflicts, inner and external, that inevitably arise in all forms of service for people.

Good supervision has four main aspects. It will offer administrative help to oversee that your work has quality and is being effectively discharged. It will be supportive in helping you to deal with your feelings and reduce your tensions and frustrations. It will help your professional development when it identifies your strengths as well as your further training needs. And it will mediate by providing a discussion forum for your concerns compared to the direction and policies of your organisation.

A conflict that often arises with supervision is that workers want emotional support, but feel their supervision is used to ensure that individual performance achieves corporate results. Once this polarisation begins to be seen it tends to become confirmed as a result of the stances the people involved impose on each other. Supervision is seldom perfect. Supervisors may not have the appropriate experience or training, sessions become relegated because of other work pressures, or essential trust has not been established.

The answer for many of these difficulties is to remember that supervision is a shared responsibility. Your support for supervision is a sure way you can stop resentments building up, and avoid difficulties from being ignored. Supervision and self-monitoring are mutually supportive practices. The issues taken to supervision are best based on your keen observation of developments and an honest approach to self. Organisations that value people also value supervision, and if you can't find shared understanding, continued work may be at a cost to you.

The different ways of self-monitoring all help to supervise self, reduce stress, and ensure well-being.

Melanie was a Teaching Assistant who attended one of my training courses. She had been engaged to provide 1:1 support in class for a young pupil who lived in a local children's home run by an organisation that specialised in provision for severely abused children. Her appointment at the school came about because the school insisted on this support before it would admit the child. Her post was paid for by the child's home Local Authority, and although she had been 'appointed' by the school it did not then see any responsibility to her as the work was not 'educational'. This was proving very stressful to her as she was coping with a lot of disturbed behaviour and transferred emotion from the child, and her line management was lacking, and without any form appropriate to her needs.

I explained about professional supervision and advised her to approach the local area manager of the children's home organisation with the stance that the child's placement and her job would only be sustainable if she got appropriate help. I reasoned this would be the best source of support for her, and had the potential to make therapeutic links between 'home' and school.

Melanie obtained fortnightly supervision during the school day provided by the 'home' manager. She was overjoyed at her own assertion, and the support provided then made it possible for her to continue her job.

Personal development contract (10)

Employment is a two-way contract and process, and there should be discussion points for issues. This may be part of appraisal, or when opportunities arise. Don't disappear into the woodwork. Make use of any appraisal, including supervision. Training arrangements should start from your personal self-appraisal about your development needs. This should not be something you just dip in and out of.

At any one time, as well as the work in hand, have some training or experience goals, or ideas about job enrichment as a way of sustaining freshness and interest, and of finding new viewpoints. The rationales are that your widened experience and perspective will enable you to carry out your prime task with improved confidence and ability. These are also the things that make a difference if you do decide you wish to move on or work elsewhere, and help you see if you are well placed at present.

Be questioning of what it means if your employer or supervisor is not sensitive to you about training or professional development, or is not willing to encourage how you and your colleagues may support each other in such pursuits. Be equally questioning if there are others more favoured, or people who seem to manipulate the system so that they are always at conferences and other jollies, particularly if they leave a workload to be carried.

Our culture still values modesty, and we do not readily draw attention to our personal achievements. The quiet stoic plodding on uncomplaining, and un-thanked, remains an icon. Yet work that is unseen cannot be appreciated, and to be passed over if you wish to be selected is not good for your self-esteem. Nor is it helpful, or just, to see a colleague carry away the accolades for something you began, and resentment and anger can begin here.

It is important to find ways to flag up instances when you are pleased with your work with a quiet assertion of what you have achieved. When you catch your supervisor in the corridor, or at coffee make sure your update includes items of good news and achievements as well as the problems. Keep a personal record so it is to hand to draw upon at times of appraisal, or if you need to compose a CV.

It is important to remember that the processes you hold as relevant for clients will also work for you. If your modesty or insecurity means that you deny or make light of the things that you have done well, then you are reinforcing a message to yourself. The message is, 'I do not value what I have done'. Do that day after day and what will that do to your self-esteem? Do recognise what you have done well, as there are plenty of times when otherwise no-one else would notice, and from time to time give yourself a pat on the back and organise a self-treat, you will have earned it.

Ask clients to let your managers know when they are particularly satisfied. Analyse how you made an achievement and raise it as a staff development or service issue, perhaps offer to use it to demonstrate a point at a staff meeting or training occasion. If you supervise, let people know when they have done well.

John provided a peripatetic service to institutions scattered around the county. The service was always under financial pressure, but was valued by service users. When John's work went particularly well he always asked that the head of the institution let his service chief know. This served two purposes. It built up valuable case evidence in support of the service, and flagged up examples of John's work that would benefit him when he was appraised.

Assertive recognition of what you do well is important to your career. Professional assertiveness is a valuable means to develop service quality.

Getting more for self (11)

Three things are important:

1. To recognise when you benefit from the processes that exist in your work.

2. To understand how you benefit.

3. To realise this is appropriate, welcome the process, and support it for oneself and others.

Getting more for oneself usually only happens by asking for it. There should be no false modesty. The thrust of many recent reports, including the Quality Protects – Social Care initiative, emphasise the importance of a well-trained and well-supported workforce. Having a clear sense of your own professional development or training needs is a very desirable key professional trait.

People who claim to know about personality development often hold that 'a person must first learn to love and care for oneself before they can care for others'. They call on self-esteem theory, on ideas like the caretaker self, and notions of the 'inner child' to support their ideas. Although this is generally true, it is possible to meet one's own needs when providing these first for others, a sort of needs met by proxy. I have seen this operate, for example, with a young man who mothered others, and was good at this, precisely because it was what he himself had most missed as a child. Eventually he trained as a psychiatric nurse.

It is a well-observed phenomenon that many people in the caring professions themselves had a past, which included difficulty, trauma or deprivation. This is an experience, which has been overcome, but remains as a touchstone for the way the person is empathetic, or expert in meeting or understanding the particular needs of others. Some people are able to openly acknowledge this, with others it is difficult to see what may be the intrinsic rewards in the work they take on. Equally, there may be unfortunate outcomes when carers are unable to attend to their own needs.

When Steve was seventeen years old he suddenly began to unleash considerable and indiscriminate violence. For many years he had been the only carer at home for his mother, who was prone to quite dramatic psychotic episodes, and he had relinquished or missed much of his earlier childhood, and now his proper passage into autonomous adulthood seemed barred by the links and self-obligations between him and his mother. His process of resolving this, understanding himself, and finding detachment from his mother, necessitated considerable support and expertise. Alternative accommodation was found and counselling was provided for him. With this Steve became stable, and he gained self-insight and was able to plan for his own future

---

People who will readily analyse and see the forces at work in the life of their clients are not always so keen to acknowledge their own needs or pressure to develop. Yet their closeness to this process in others can mean unresolved personal dynamics may be exposed and must be resolved if they are not to hinder their work. The alternative is to bury or carry personal issues, and they may be like time bombs waiting to be triggered, or if never resolved the person becomes emotionally stuck.

A man who was gifted with many skills worked well with quite disturbed adolescent boys in a special residential school. One of the things he held very important, even rigidly, was behaviour at mealtimes. He was very keen that these were sociable occasions. He ensured that manners on his table were good, and intervened swiftly if there was any conflict emerging between the boys. There was always lively talk on his table, which was popular, and invariably it was one of the last tables to be cleared.

I had occasion to be invited into his home. There was no dining table in the house. His family sat eating tea, with trays on their knees, watching TV.

Although subconscious personal issues motivated his approach to the work he did, they remained unconfronted by him, and he did not acknowledge the source of some of his passions. A few years later this man had to leave in unfortunate circumstances which partly arose as he had become distanced from developments in the establishment. It had changed, but he could not.

Unfortunately, workers are often not aware of the sources of their feelings, they may be providing for clients what they themselves lacked or did not have when needed, or be dealing with transferences (see earlier this chapter). This can motivate or demotivate. A particular event can leave a professional person in turmoil as they confront an issue of some sort that is 'too close to home' and as yet unresolved, or barely recognised in their self.

Personal responses vary. Anger or jealousy of clients is quite common but seldom recognised, and usually subconsciously suppressed. Young clients may have better opportunities or material provision than the worker at the same age. Other clients may be viewed as people who do not value what they are given, or are receiving better than they deserve. Jealousy may be an unfocused and generalised feeling. If so, this may indicate the worker's own emotional needs for attention and support are probably not adequately met.

People whose work is in any way therapeutic, be this nursing, teaching, caring, or similar fields, will meet issues relevant to themselves. They will find themselves in process to some degree. It is important to allow for this. It may mean you, or a colleague, are at times very uncertain. The uncertainty may be about a career decision, the quality of work, or the degree of personal involvement needed. Often development in self-awareness is prevented by the denial or suppression of feeling for self. It may seem selfish to do this in the face of strongly contrasting client situations. What is not realised is that although material circumstances or personal situations may differ, client from professional, human feelings are universal.

Professional people often expect too much of themselves and this shows as:

• Not admitting to own feelings or suppressing these.

• Denying own emotional needs.

- Denying own physical needs.
- Being too self-critical.
- Not accepting occasional failure.
- Not celebrating things done well.
- Finding praise and thanks difficult to accept.
- Emotional rigidity.

A client who was making a real effort, but experienced difficulty on occasion would not be so harshly judged. No professional person is perfect either. Good supervision will provide a balance. Supervision should support a worker in process, as would other support services such as access to counselling. If you have not got this available when you might need it, begin to ask for it now. If it is your responsibility to others, you must ensure it.

One important task of supervision is to help acknowledge when others or the supervisee is developing. This may mean recognising an issue that may need some help to see through, or simply when a little more tolerance is needed for a while. If this process of self-development is prevented it will have personal and organisational costs as the true self are compromised. The worker may lose effectiveness, or even become antagonistic to a previous purpose. Behaviour traits most at risk are those such as tolerance, empathy, and placidity.

Conflict in personal life can result from work. Difficult interpersonal work is supported best when there is tolerance at home from friends and relatives who have some understanding of the pressures the work brings. Disharmony with partners and friends may result from the changes that happen in self. Either the difficulties of process need support and it is not given, or the person develops in ways that distance them from people to whom they were once close. This may mean letting others know about your process difficulties, possibly at home and certainly at work. Asking opens up possibilities, firstly to self as any denial is now past, and secondly it makes a response from colleagues more likely to occur, as formal supervision, or more informally.

Personal safety includes psychological consideration as well as concern about physical harm. Unsafe colleagues will reject feelings and may reject a viewpoint in a manner that aggrandises them and puts others down. This may make co-workers anxious or depressed, or defensive and angry. Safe colleagues are those you can rely on to discuss with you, and support you, with any concern you take to them. You will not feel the need to defend your feelings, or hide them from view. If your colleagues share your views about how to be mutually supportive there will be a system and support structures that are available to yourself and colleagues at times of need.

Be cautious about co-counselling or a co-therapist system. Because these systems often rely on peer colleagues they may play into the reinforcement of a viewpoint, or be limited, even detrimental, to psychological health if anxiety or preoccupation is shared rather than processed.

Being sensitive to yourself may well open up sensitivities to others you did not know you had, and your power of intuition may grow.

Intuition is a sense about a person or a situation that seems unsupported by what can immediately be observed, or substantiated. Intuition stems from some logic or knowledge that is only available on an unconscious level. People who always 'guess right' are usually those who are fully in tune with self, and confident to trust their instincts or intuitions. The more a person feels balanced and confident, the more certain the value of their intuitions will be. Trusting intuitions is trusting self.

Understanding personal processes supports professional development.
Understand that the work you do will change you.

Self-esteem concepts applied (12)

It may be helpful to view 'self-esteem' as 'personal significance'. This means it does not matter how high or lowly your position is, you matter to the people around you, and you have their love and respect for who you are and what you do, whatever that is. In this situation you are less vulnerable to transferences and self-doubts.

But the catch is that personal significance is dependent on what others project back to you. Despite how 'good' a person you might actually be, or yet become, others have to perceive this and reflect it back, and you are dependent on the psychological health of your colleagues, friends, and family.

This now leads to the double catch. How your clients fare depends on what you project back to them. Human potential thrives on positive regard. Your client's personal significance will grow if they are personally significant to you, not clinically or 'professionally' but deep in your heart you know and believe it as a tenet of faith in humanity. It is a positive cycle of regard.

High self-esteem makes a person safer. It correlates with the sort of positive outlook that resists seeing self as a victim of events, and resists the thought processes that lead into spirals of depression or negativity. And it presents a more robust personal demeanour to would-be aggressors.

Good personal significance reduces the potential to feel aggressive as it correlates with an outlook on life that does not seek dysfunctional rewards.

I hope the ideas presented in this last chapter have centred your thinking about self, and I believe are important for one good reason. This is that people, who are affective and effective in transforming the lives of others, also feel positive about themselves. A great deal of psychological research has had very clear results on this one point.

The congruency here should never be overlooked. A person whose ideas and wishes are in sympathy with their organisation enjoys compatibility with it, and with their colleagues. If this is your situation it will allow you the best opportunity to contribute, which in turn

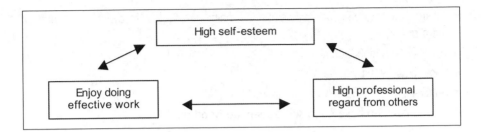

feeds into your personal significance cycle. Look to see if you are valued and given the encouragement to be yourself. Anything less than this means some amount of compromise, the reality for most people.

Important personal checks are that you look for this congruency in self, and in your organisation. The evaluation you make is about any compromise, and if there is one, can you live with it, or can you change it?

- The best way to cope with aggression of any kind and from any source starts by feeling positive about oneself.

- Safe systems, safe colleagues, and safe forms of support make you safe.

- People who feel safe are not aggressive.

My intention has been that this book has helped you to:

- Maximise your personal, physical, and professional safety.

- Recognise that responding to aggression requires thoughtful consideration and a planned response just as with any other problem behaviour.

- Use new techniques and skills to minimise the potential for aggression in others.

- Know how to defuse situations and set up more caring responses.

- Know how to analyse your workplace systems and physical environment for the benefit of reducing aggressive events.

- Improve your responses by feeling more secure and being in control in the situations you get caught up in.

- Have a new alertness to possible sources of aggression in yourself and others, and recognise them when they are disguised.

- Know better how to expect your workplace and colleagues to be right and good, and be open to comment and process.

- Be more alert to practice in your workplace that may be dysfunctional.

- Have more certainty about how injustices may be dealt with.

- Ensure your personal achievements and gains are noted following your rightful self-assertion.
- Trust your intuition better.
- Know better what you do well.
- Understand the value of your self-approval.

Professionals who have good self-esteem do good work.

Contact Information

Injury at work:
For HSE publications, including Violence in the Education Sector; and for their catalogue:
HSE Books, PO Box 1999, Sudbury, Suffolk CO10 2WA. Tel: 01787 881165. Website:
www.hsebooks.co.uk

Health and Safety Executive national helpline: 0541 545500

Government Information on violence at work: www.doh.gov.uk/violencetaskforce

The Suzy Lamplugh Trust for a copy of its useful pamphlet *Personal Safety at Work –
Guidance for all Employees*
Suzy Lamplugh Trust, 14 East Sheen Avenue, London SW14 8AS. Tel: 0180 876 0305

**Counselling and consultancy in the event of a major crisis or traumatic event,
especially in schools:**
The Centre for Crisis Management and Education, Roselyn House, 93 Old Newtown
Road, Newbury, Berkshire RG14 7DE. Tel: 01635 30644

Conspiracy at work:
'Freedom to Care', PO Box 125, West Molesey, Surrey KT8 1YE. Tel: 0181 224 1022
*This is the premier support organisation, knowledgeable on relevant legislation, and in
the range of expertise and experience it offers in support after an event; but better to
allow it to guide on the issues as they develop. FtC proactively point the way with
relevant publications and a keenness to promote ethical accountability.*

Mainly consultancy:
Public Concern at Work, Lincoln Inn House, 42 Kingsway, London WC2B B46EN.
Tel: 0171 404 6609

Bullying at work:
For a fact pack and consultancy from 'Success Unlimited' and Tim Field:
National Workplace Bullying Advice Line: 01235 834548 (office hours)
PO Box 77, Wantage, Oxfordshire OX12 8YP

Imperative. Bullying Helpline: 0181 885 1677 (weekdays and Sat am) and 01983 856379 (weekdays 8–10 pm)

In Schools:

DfES: 'A Legal Toolkit for Schools: tackling abuse, threats and violence towards members of the school community'. Tel: 0845 602 2260, or www.teachernet.gov.uk/Management/ Working . . . With . . . Others/safeschools/

For children at risk of harm:

Childline: 0800 1111 (24-hour freephone)

Kidscape: (large SAE for advice on child bullying), 152 Buckingham Palace Road, London SW1W 9TR. Tel: 0171 730 3300

Forum on Children and Violence, c/o National Children's Bureau, 8 Wakeley Street, London EC1V 7QE. Tel: 0171 843 6309

Victim support:

Victim Support. The national charity, the local phone number is in BT phonebooks.

Other:

Your professional or trades union, contact national HQ or local representative.

Your local Citizens Advice Bureaux.

Social Care Association, Thornton House, Hook Road, Surbiton, Surrey KT6 5AN. Tel: 0181 397 1411

The association produces a range of booklets on good workplace practice, including Dealing with Violence in Care Settings, and Harassment, Discrimination and Bullying.

National Countering Bullying Unit, University of Wales Institute Cardiff, Cyn Coed Campus, Cyn Coed Road, Cardiff CF2 6XD. Tel: 01222 506 781

Health and Safety Executive, Rose Court, 2 Southwark Bridge, London SE1 9HS. Tel: 0171 717 6000

HSE books and reports: PO Box 1999, Sudbury, Suffolk CO10 6FS

References

Abrams, J. (1995) *Reclaiming the Inner Child*. Thorsons. (The therapeutic leitmotif, essential awareness for sensitive work with self and others.)

Bresler, F. (1995) *Law Without a Lawyer*. Sinclair Stevenson.

Cava, R. (1990) *Dealing with Difficult People*. Piatkus. (Excellent advice on managing difficult colleagues or customers.)

Clifton, J. and Serdar, H. (2000) *Bully Off*. Russell House Publishing. (How to respond to bullying at work.)

Dawes, M. (1999) *Managing the Monkey*. The Therapist Ltd. Cromwell Press. (How to defuse conflicts and respond to dangerous people in the workplace.)

Field, L. (1993) *Creating Self-esteem*. Element. (A practical, wise, self-help guide.)

Field, T. (1996) *Bully in Sight*. Success Unlimited. (How to predict, resist, challenge and combat workplace bullying. Book list. Comprehensive contact list of varied and relevant organisations.)

Glass, L. (1991) *Confident Conversation*. Piatkus. (Relevant, wide-ranging, but a bit gushy in tone.)

Goleman, D. (1996) *Emotional Intelligence*. Bloomsbury Publishing. (Useful on the physiology of anger, generally relevant as background illumination to many issues and responses.)

Harris, T. (1995) *I'm OK You're OK*. Arrow. (Relationship theory of transational analysis.)

Hunt, G. (1995) *Whistleblowing in the Health Service*. Arnold.

Lamplugh, D. and Pagan, B. (1996) *Personal Safety for Schools*. Arena. (Has wider application, training routines within text, some advice about personal safety and responses to threat, a very useful book list, government publications, contact addresses. Companion books on personal safety for social workers, for health care workers.)

LeDoux, J. (1998) *The Emotional Brain*. Weidenfeld and Nicolson.

Makarenko, A. (1951) *The Road to Life*. Foreign Language Publishing House.

McCormack, M. (1985) *What They Don't Teach You at Harvard Business School*. Guild. (How to negotiate.)

Morris, D. (1967) *The Naked Ape*. Cape.

O'Connor, J. and Seymour, J. (1990) *Introducing NLP*. Thorsons. (As good an introduction to neuro-linguistic programming as any other.)

Pease, A. (1995) *Body Language*. Sheldon Press. (Useful book list on interpersonal behaviour.)

Perry, B. www.quolkids.com, www.tdprs.state.tx.us, and *Time Magazine*, 3 Feb. 1997; *Sunday Times* 7 Sept. 2003.

Redl, F. and Wineman, D. (1965) *Controls From Within: Techniques for The Treatment of the Aggressive Child*. The Free Press (Macmillan). (The seminal work.)

Schaef, A.W. (1992) *Beyond Therapy, Beyond Science*. Harper. (About people in process.)

Thompson, N. (2000) *Tackling Bullying and Harassment in the Workplace*. Pepar Publications. (Also Training Pack: www.pepar.co.uk)

Wescott, P. (1995) *How to Get What You Want*. Bloomsbury. (Self-assertion, self-help paperback.)